Ronald Reagan's Journey

Ronald Reagan's Journey

Democrat to Republican

Edward M. Yager

ROWMAN & LITTLEFIELD PUBLISHERS, INC.
Lanham • Boulder • New York • Toronto • Oxford

ROWMAN & LITTLEFIELD PUBLISHERS, INC.

Published in the United States of America
by Rowman & Littlefield Publishers, Inc.
A wholly owned subsidary of The Rowman & Littlefield Publishing Group, Inc.
4501 Forbes Boulevard, Suite 200, Lanham, Maryland 20706
www.rowmanlittlefield.com

PO Box 317
Oxford
OX2 9RU, UK

British Library Cataloguing in Publication Information Available

Library of Congress Cataloging-in-Publication Data

Yager, Edward M., 1951–
  Ronald Reagan's journey : Democrat to Republican / Edward M. Yager.
      p. cm.
  Includes bibliographical references and index.
  ISBN-13: 978-0-7425-4420-8 (cloth : alk. paper)
  ISBN-10: 0-7425-4420-6 (cloth : alk. paper)
  ISBN-13: 978-0-7425-4421-5 (pbk. : alk. paper)
  ISBN-10: 0-7425-4421-4 (pbk. : alk. paper)
  1. Reagan, Ronald. 2. Presidents—United States—Biography. 3. United States—
Politics and government—1981–1989. I. Title.

  E877.Y34 2006
  973.927092—dc22   2005032399

Printed in the United States of America

⊗™ The paper used in this publication meets the minimum requirements of
American National Standard for Information Sciences—Permanence of Paper for
Printed Library Materials, ANSI/NISO Z39.48-1992.

To my mother-in-law,
Esther Katie Monschke Hughes.
Her journey through life has inspired
countless numbers throughout the world.

I have spent most of my life as a Democrat. I recently have seen fit to follow another course. I believe that the issues confronting us cross party lines. . . . You and I have a rendezvous with destiny.

—Ronald Reagan, *A Time for Choosing*, October 27, 1964

For most of my adult life I was a Democrat. Born and raised a Democrat. I, too, came to the moment of discomfort with the party that I had grown up with—the realization that I could no longer lend support or go down the line with them. For those of you who have made this decision, I understand something of the emotional wrench that accompanies such a decision. It was strange to me to find out at the moment of parting, what an ingrained loyalty there is, and how very difficult it is to sever the ties and to walk away from that party and turn to the party which you have always opposed. But, I don't believe that any person, recognizing what is going on in America today, can legitimately do anything else.

—Ronald Reagan, campaign speech on behalf of
Republican Candidate Charlton H. Lyons, Lafayette, Louisiana, 1964

I guess it was in 1960, the year Richard Nixon ran against John F. Kennedy for the presidency, that I completed my political journey from liberal Democrat to dedicated Republican.

—Ronald Reagan, *An American Life*

Contents

Acknowledgments

I am indebted to many people for their kind assistance on this project. I wish to thank my wonderful wife, Marie. She has provided the encouragement that only she can provide. I also thank my children, Kristina and Mark, for their sustained support and patience.

Two individuals provided invaluable assistance. They both took an early interest in this project and worked with me on it for three years. Professor emeritus and former colleague Edward Kearny reviewed each chapter thoroughly. His suggested revisions were consistently on target and enhanced the quality of this book. I enjoyed our "working" dinners to discuss revisions after each chapter had been written and reviewed. Mr. Joshua Sampson, M.P.A., provided outstanding research assistance. Even after leaving Western Kentucky University, Joshua continued to relay articles and books to me. Thank you, Joshua!

Three scholars with special expertise on Ronald Reagan and the Reagan presidency were very helpful. Paul Kengor, Andrew Busch, and Martin Anderson have all published outstanding books on Reagan and the Reagan presidency. I am honored that they reviewed my work and provided many helpful suggestions to improve its quality.

During the summer of 2002, I conducted research at the Ronald Reagan Presidential Library in Simi Valley, California. Two archivists, Diane Barrie and Gregory Cumming, were particularly helpful in locating documents and answering my countless questions. They, and the staff at the Library, made my visit to Simi Valley very enjoyable, as well as productive.

I also thank Western Kentucky University. Western provided me with a summer fellowship grant to undertake research at the Reagan Library and a one-semester sabbatical to write a major portion of this book. In particular, I am grateful to librarian Rosemary Meszaros for her considerable research support, and to President Gary Ransdell and Political Science Department head Saundra Ardrey for their administrative and moral support.

The Rowman & Littlefield Publishing Group has been an ideal organization to work with on this project. I consider my professional contacts at Rowman & Littlefield, Laura Gottlieb and Andrew Boney, to be friends as well as partners in this work. Their wise and timely assistance has been helpful and greatly appreciated.

Although many have assisted with this project, the author assumes all responsibility for whatever deficiencies exist.

Introduction

Ronald Reagan's journey on this earth ended June 5, 2004. His life was eulo-gized by world leaders in the National Cathedral in Washington, D.C., as people throughout the world reflected on his life and his presidency. Future generations in America and in other countries will learn that, whether they agree or disagree with his policies, Ronald Reagan was a champion for indi-vidual freedom in the latter half of the twentieth century, and he played a key role in promoting the expansion of political and economic freedom worldwide. But now his work is done, and his body rests in Simi Valley, Cal-ifornia. His journey on earth is complete.

Ronald Reagan viewed the passage of his life in two distinct ways. In one, he viewed his entire life as a journey through time. But in another way, he viewed his life as many shorter journeys that combined to make up his life's overall journey. Reagan began to think in these terms relatively early in life. When he was only seventeen years old, Reagan wrote a poem that was in-cluded in his high school yearbook, *The Dixonian*. The poem, "Life," reveals Reagan's depth and eloquence at a young age. The poem also reveals that he thought of life as a journey.

Life
I wonder what it's all about, and why
We suffer so, when little things go wrong?
We make our life a struggle,
When life should be a song.

1

Our troubles break and drench us,
Like spray on the cleaving prow
Of some trim Gloucester schooner
As it dips in a graceful bow.

Our troubles break and drench us
But like that cleaving prow,
The wind will fan and dry us.
And we'll watch some other bow.

But why does sorrow drench us
When our fellow passes on?
He's just exchanged life's dreary dirge
For an eternal life of song

What is the inborn trait
That frowns on a life of song?
That makes us weep at the journey's end,
When the journey was oft-times wrong?

Weep when we reach the door
That opens to let us in,
And brings to us eternal peace
As it closes again on sin.

Millions have gone before us,
And millions will come behind.
So why do we curse and fight
At a fate both wise and kind.

We hang onto a jaded life
A life full of sorrow and pain.
A life that warps and breaks us,
And we try to run through it again.[1]

At the other end of Reagan's life, at eighty-three, and not long after being diagnosed with Alzheimer's disease, Reagan composed his "Last Letter to America." The letter was delivered to the nation on November 5, 1994, just ten years before his death. Reagan eloquently conveyed his condition to the nation and once again described his life as a journey, and his Alzheimer's condition, which would take him to the end of his life, as a journey in itself. In the letter, Reagan wrote,

Last Letter to America[2]

My fellow Americans, I have recently been told that I am one of the millions of Americans who will be afflicted with Alzheimer's disease.

Upon learning this news, Nancy and I had to decide whether as private citizens we would keep this a private matter or whether we would make this news known in a public way. In the past, Nancy suffered from breast cancer and I had my cancer surgeries. We found through our open disclosures we were able to raise public awareness. We were happy that as a result, many more people underwent testing. They were treated in early stages and able to return to normal, healthy lives.

So now we feel it is important to share it with you. In opening our hearts, we hope this might promote greater awareness of this condition. Perhaps it will encourage a clearer understanding of the individuals and families who are affected by it. At the moment I feel just fine. I intend to live the remainder of the years God gives me on this earth doing the things I have always done. *I will continue to share life's journey with my beloved Nancy and my family.* I plan to enjoy the great outdoors and stay in touch with my friends and supporters.

Unfortunately, as Alzheimer's disease progresses, the family often bears a heavy burden. I only wish there was some way I could spare Nancy this painful experience. When the time comes, I am confident that with your help she will face it with faith and courage.

In closing, let me thank you, the American people, for giving me the great honor of allowing me to serve as your president. When the Lord calls me home, whenever that day may be, I will leave with the greatest love for this country of ours and eternal optimism for its future.

I now begin the journey that will lead me into the sunset of my life. I know that for America there will always be a bright dawn ahead.

Thank you, my friends. May God always bless you.

Sincerely,
Ronald Reagan

In his letter to the American people, Reagan states that he "will continue to share life's journey" and "now I begin the journey." The letter clearly expresses both meanings in which Reagan viewed his journey through life: life itself as one long journey and distinct periods of life as separate journeys. Consistent with this latter dimension of thought, Reagan's farewell address to the nation reveals that he thought of his presidency as a distinct journey through time. After discussing America's renewed commitment to freedom during the 1980s, Reagan said, "It's been quite a *journey this decade,* and we held together through some stormy seas. And at the end, together, we are reaching our destination."[3]

Reagan's use of the word *journey* was not simply to utilize an effective metaphor to advance an argument. The word conveyed, in a very real sense, Reagan's underlying belief in the purpose and the meaning of human life. From an early age, Reagan held the view that each human life was divinely ordered. This was earnestly taught to young Reagan by his devout mother, Nelle. In her Christian theology, informed by her Protestant denomination, God has a plan for each life. The doctrine of divine providence therefore helps explain more fully why Reagan saw his life, and different periods of his life, as a journey linked to the unfolding of a divine plan.

This knowledge also deepens our understanding of Reagan's frequent references to John Winthrop, the early American Puritan. Reagan often referred to Winthrop's description of America as a "City upon a Hill" and its lesson about America's duty to preserve freedom not only for America but for the world. Less well known but contained within Winthrop's Puritan theology was the message of divine providence over nations and individuals. Reagan believed this message and gave it expression in his speeches and letters by using words such as *journey* and *destiny*.

A journey implies a destiny, and Reagan often used the word *destiny* in his speeches and letters. Perhaps his most famous use of the word was contained in his 1964 "Time for Choosing" speech on behalf of Barry Goldwater. Toward the end of the speech, Reagan referred to America's destiny in the world. He quoted Churchill as saying that "the destiny of man is not measured by material computation. When great forces are on the move in the world, we learn we are spirits—not animals. . . . There is something going on in time and space, and beyond time and space, which, whether we like it or not, spells duty." And then Reagan concluded, "You and I have a rendezvous with destiny."[4] The line was borrowed from FDR's 1936 speech in Philadelphia in which he accepted the Democratic nomination, but it nonetheless captured Reagan's views. Ten years later, Reagan again used the word *destiny* in a lesser-known speech. In his address "We Will Be a City upon a Hill," Reagan articulated the Puritan view that "we cannot escape our destiny, nor should we try to do so. The leadership of the free world was thrust upon us two centuries ago in that little hall of Philadelphia."[5] A little over one year later, Reagan said in an address that "we did not seek world leadership; it was thrust upon us. It has been our destiny almost from the first moment this land was settled. If we fail to keep our rendezvous with destiny or, as John Winthrop said in 1630, 'Deal falsely with our God,' we shall be made a 'story and byword throughout the world.'"[6]

This is a small sample of Reagan's speeches that reveals his providential views about America's role in the world and in human history. At a different level, Reagan held the same providential views about the ordering of individual lives. Individuals as well as nations had a journey through time, and both ultimately had a destiny to be reached. And, like nations, individuals had the awesome and mysterious gift of freedom to shape that journey and that destiny. Reagan believed that the power of free choice, working together mysteriously with Providence, shaped the journeys of individuals and nations.

This book is about one such journey taken by Ronald Reagan between 1945 and 1962. It was one of many journeys Reagan took throughout his life, yet it was one of the most important. It was a journey that set him on the course to his political career and then on to the presidency. This pivotal journey contained a diversity of life experiences that moved Reagan from being a Democrat to being a Republican.

In Reagan's view, his journey was not an ideological sojourn to conservatism. At the time, Reagan did not see himself undergoing an ideological change; he thought, instead, that he was simply responding to various threats to American freedom. He viewed himself as a citizen warning his countrymen of the dangers of Communism and an encroaching federal government.

Ultimately, Reagan would announce upon his switch to the Republican Party that he had not left the Democratic Party, but rather the Democratic Party had left him. In Reagan's mind, the Democratic Party had left him by departing from its Jeffersonian beliefs in limited and decentralized government. As Andrew Busch has noted, "[Reagan] typically explained his abandonment of the Democratic Party, made formal in 1962, by reference to the Democrats' abandonment of Jeffersonian principles of limited government."[7] For many Democrats, New Deal liberalism was a pivotal turning point that prompted their defection to the Republican Party. Even Wendell Willkie, the Republican nominee for the presidency in 1940, was a former Democrat who defected to the Republican Party shortly before his nomination. Willkie and many other former Democrats, such as Reagan's older brother Neil, advanced arguments that the Democratic Party had betrayed its Jeffersonian roots in limited government. Other Democrats, however, emphasized Jeffersonian beliefs in an attempt to justify a greater federal presence in American society.

Ronald Reagan, however, did not immediately leave the Democratic Party after 1932. Instead, he remained a Democrat and defended FDR and the New Deal for many years. Reagan's political development from 1945 to 1962 is therefore crucial to understanding his switch from the Democratic Party to the Republican Party.

After World War II and his return to civilian life in 1945, Reagan still considered himself a liberal New Deal Democrat. Over the next seventeen years, however, Reagan would gradually come to believe that liberalism undermined America's highest value—individual freedom. On foreign policy, Reagan would learn that liberals were often naively "soft" toward Soviet Communism. On domestic policy, Reagan would discover that liberals actively promoted a growing federal bureaucracy. In both cases, American freedom was threatened. Reagan did not consider liberalism synonymous with the Democratic Party, but he did conclude that the heart of liberalism was to be found there. As Reagan moved away from liberalism, he therefore moved away from the Democratic Party.

Reagan increasingly found that the political beliefs and values he acquired from 1945 to 1962 simply no longer had a home in the Democratic Party. His newly developed views were far from a perfect fit with the Republican Party, but the Republicans offered a more hospitable domain for him than the Democrats did. Although he had been campaigning for Republicans for years, Reagan finally changed his party registration from Democrat to Republican in 1962. He would run as a Republican candidate for governor of California four years later.

Ronald Reagan's journey from Democrat to Republican has been described anecdotally by Reagan in his two autobiographies as well as by many of the Reagan biographies. To my knowledge, no work has systematically examined this very important period of political development in Ronald Reagan's life. The journey metaphor is therefore a fitting and appropriate one for a more thorough review of this period in the life of Ronald Reagan. By his frequent use of the metaphor in speeches and letters, Reagan himself would likely approve.

However, we need to explore further the meaning of the concept of "journey" before proceeding to discuss this particular journey of Reagan's. We have done that to some extent by recognizing that Reagan often associated the words *destiny* and *destination* with his understanding of life's journeys, but a journey implies many attributes. For instance, it includes new circumstances as a journey unfolds. A journey often means meeting new people, passing by new locations, and constantly gathering new information for the sojourner's evaluation. A journey is a dynamic process. It is full of change. It is, perhaps more than anything else, a *learning* process for the sojourner. The journey constantly provides new information that prompts the sojourner to choose. He must choose to remain on the same path or to move to a different path as he proceeds to his destination.

In Ronald Reagan's journey, the core values he acquired in his youth provided something of a moral compass for his later journey. Those core values, and their importance to his later political development, are discussed in chapter 1. Chapter 2 closely examines the changing circumstances he faced in Hollywood immediately after World War II. Those circumstances brought Reagan face to face with Communist attempts to undermine American freedom. Because of his reevaluation of the Communist threat, his views toward Communism hardened in response. His belief that Communism had to be defeated rather than tolerated came largely out of this early postwar experience with Communists in Hollywood. Chapter 3 examines how Reagan gradually began to relinquish his New Deal beliefs and argue instead that the federal government should have a more limited domestic role. This phase of Reagan's journey occurred during the 1950s, and most of it came after his marriage to Nancy in 1952. Reagan was learning from a variety of sources at this time, but his General Electric experience from 1954 to 1962 was particularly important. Chapter 4 focuses on important relationships during Reagan's journey. Family members and friends often debated politics with Reagan, and they advanced Republican arguments to him repeatedly. Reagan did not dismiss these arguments, partly because he valued and trusted the people advancing them, but neither did he convert to them easily. Chapter 5 explores important intellectual influences Reagan encountered during the 1950s. Reagan's journey occurred during a renaissance of thought that opposed Communism and statism. Major intellectuals were writing about many of the issues important to Reagan at this time, and Reagan read many of their works. Whittaker Chambers's *Witness* and Nobel Prize–winning economist Friedrich Hayek's *The Road to Serfdom* were among the books read by Reagan, and their influence on him is examined in some detail.

These five chapters do not exhaust all of the influences on Reagan during his journey from Democrat to Republican. They are, however, the most important ones. Even among these five influences, the first three were the primary ones, while the influences of family, friends, and intellectuals were secondary and largely reinforcing. Reagan learned fundamentally from his direct experience. Family, friends, and intellectuals only helped to confirm conclusions that he had come to earlier. Finally, the distinctive influences identified and systematically examined in this book were, in many instances, interacting together to influence Reagan. They were part of an experiential milieu that provided dynamic changes to Reagan's understanding of the political world. For the purpose of providing greater clarity to the reader, however, each influence has been identified and separated from the others for a deeper examination.

The concluding chapter of this book, chapter 6, examines the larger meaning of Reagan's journey from Democrat to Republican. The significance of the journey did not end with its completion in 1962. Rather, the lessons

Reagan discovered during his sojourn became the defining elements of his presidency. During his presidency, Reagan effectively used the bully pulpit to advance those lessons he had learned decades earlier. The concluding chapter argues that the Reagan presidency cannot be properly understood and evaluated without significant attribution to Reagan's spiritual, political, and economic beliefs.

Ronald Reagan's journey from Democrat to Republican reminds us that we each have a journey through life. Like Reagan, each of us will encounter changing circumstances that may shape our political views in the future. Will we be apathetic or will we try to learn from the journey? Reagan's life is a testament to an engaged citizen learning from life's journey.

Notes

1. Kiron Skinner, Annelise Anderson, and Martin Anderson, eds., *Reagan, in His Own Hand* (New York: Free Press, 2001), 426, emphasis added.

2. Kiron Skinner, Annelise Anderson, and Martin Anderson, eds., *Reagan: A Life in Letters* (New York: Free Press, 2003), 832–33, emphasis added.

3. Ronald Reagan, "Farewell Address to the Nation," in *Speaking My Mind* (New York: Simon & Schuster, 1989), 411, emphasis added.

4. Ronald Reagan, "A Time for Choosing," in *Speaking My Mind* (New York: Simon & Schuster, 1989), 36.

5. Ronald Reagan, "We Will Be a City upon a Hill," in *The Greatest Speeches of Ronald Reagan* (West Palm Beach, CA: NewsMax.Com, 2001), 31.

6. Ronald Reagan, "Let Them Go Their Way," *The Greatest Speeches of Ronald Reagan* (West Palm Beach, CA: NewsMax.Com, 2001), 41.

7. Andrew Busch, *Ronald Reagan and the Politics of Freedom* (Lanham, MD: Rowman & Littlefield, 2001), 6.

CHAPTER ONE

~

Early Years

Ronald Reagan was born on February 6, 1911, to Jack and Nelle Reagan in Tampico, Illinois. He was the second of two children born to the Reagans. His older brother, Neil, had been born over two years earlier in Tampico. Together, the Reagan brothers were raised in a home and community atmosphere that instilled fundamental beliefs and values about living that endured throughout their lives. These sorts of permanent beliefs and values are often referred to as "core" beliefs and values, and an understanding of young Reagan's core beliefs and values better enables us to understand his later political development.

By contrast, young Reagan's political beliefs were largely undefined and undeveloped during the 1930s and 1940s. Only in the late 1940s and continuing during the 1950s, when Reagan perceived that American freedom was being threatened by Communism and an overly intrusive federal government, would his core beliefs provoke a response. Reagan's political beliefs would then begin to take more definite shape and reveal his political philosophy.

Core Beliefs

Ronald Reagan's parents, Jack and Nelle, could hardly have been more different. He was a nominal Catholic; she was a devoted Protestant. He was a drinker; she was a teetotaler. He was an extrovert; she was an introvert. In his second autobiography, Ronald Reagan captured some of these differences when he noted, "While my father was a cynic and tended to suspect the worst of people, my mother was the opposite. She always expected to find the best in people and often did, even among the prisoners at our local jail to whom she frequently brought hot meals."[1] Reagan also said, "Although my father's attendance at Catholic Mass was sporadic, my mother seldom missed Sunday services at the Disciples of Christ Church in Dixon."[2] These and other differences between Jack and Nelle have been well documented by Reagan's biographers. For instance, in an early biography of Reagan, Lee Edwards observes, "They made quite a contrast. Jack, standing almost six feet, was tall, muscular, of swarthy complexion with thick, wavy, brown hair and blue eyes. He was outspoken, quick-tempered, a natural raconteur. She was gentle and soft-spoken. He was Catholic, an indifferent churchgoer; she was Protestant and deeply religious. He was too fond of alcohol, she was a teetotaler."[3]

These parental differences made unique and distinctive contributions to Reagan's young life. From his father, Ronald Reagan believed he learned the value of hard work and ambition, and maybe a little something about telling a story. From his mother, Reagan felt he learned the value of prayer, how to have dreams, and how to believe he could make them come true.[4] He also knew that his father pursued dreams of success through selling shoes, but he realized that his father's dreams were vanquished by consistent failure. However, young Reagan understood that these failed dreams were largely his father's own fault because of excessive drinking, not a denial of opportunity.

In fact, Jack's own philosophy of life was consistent with this assessment. Reagan observed about his father, "Among the things [Jack] passed on to me was the belief that all men and women, regardless of their color or religion, are created equal and that *individuals determine their own destiny; that is, it's largely their own ambition and hard work that determine their fate in life.*"[5] To temper this highly individualistic work ethic that Reagan received from his father, Nelle taught young Reagan that "God has a plan for everyone and that seemingly random twists of fate are all a part of His plan. . . . All things were part of God's plan, even the most disheartening setbacks, and in the end, everything worked out for the best."[6] Where Jack emphasized freedom, opportunity, and personal responsibility in life, Nelle reminded her son of divine Providence in turning failure into success. Young Reagan incorporated both teachings into his life. To a significant degree, these teachings influenced young Reagan's initiative, ambition, and success in sports announcing and acting prior to his political career. These teachings, especially his mother's, also contributed to an optimistic temperament that would later serve him well in politics.

The small Midwestern communities where Reagan was raised reinforced the basic parental values passed on to the future president. In fact, Reagan described Dixon, Illinois, as a "small universe where I learned standards and values that would guide me for the rest of my life."[7] In Dixon, Reagan learned both communitarian and individualistic values. Most notably, Reagan's community values were rooted in neighbors helping neighbors *without the help of government*. Reagan, reflecting on his experience in Dixon, observed that "almost everyone knew one another, and because they knew one another, they tended to care about each other. If a family down the street had a crisis—a death or serious illness—a neighbor brought them dinner that night. If a farmer lost his barn to a fire, his friends would pitch in and help him rebuild it."[8]

At an individual level, however, Reagan said he "learned that hard work is an essential part of life—that by and large, you don't get something for nothing—and that America was a place that offered unlimited opportunity to those who did work hard. I learned to admire risk takers and entrepreneurs, be they farmers or small merchants, who went to work and took risks to build something for themselves and their children, pushing at the boundaries of their lives to make them better."[9] An early Reagan biographer, Bill Boyarsky, made a similar observation about Reagan many years before Reagan's autobiography *An American Life*. Boyarsky noted that "Reagan loves the small towns, admires the conservative men who run them and looks back on his youth with fond memories. . . . He was shaped by the small towns of the Midwest, and that explains in large part the simple moral and conservative approach he brought to public life . . . convinced, as his father said, [that] all men were created equal and [that] man's own ambition determines what happens to him the rest of his life."[10] And though Reagan's father emphasized human equality and individual responsibility, it was Reagan's mother, Nelle, with her sunny optimism rooted in her religious faith, who would inspire Reagan to follow his dreams to his ultimate destiny. Reagan expressed this lifelong and strongly held core belief when he argued, "We all want the chance to work at a job of our own choosing and to be fairly rewarded for it and the opportunity to control our own destiny. . . . The dreams of people may differ, but everyone wants their dreams to come true. . . . And America, above all places, gives us the freedom to do that, the freedom to reach out and make our dreams come true."[11] This is a very strong statement by Ronald Reagan, and it is revealing. It captures the simplicity of Reagan's core belief that human freedom allows people to dream, to pursue their dreams, and to perhaps realize those dreams. This was not only Reagan's *belief*—it was also his experience. He would live out his dreams, which would serve to increase his appreciation for American freedom.

Political Beliefs

However, the family and community values instilled in young Reagan did not develop into Republican political beliefs. Reagan was raised in a family that strongly identified with the Democratic Party and Franklin Roosevelt's New Deal program during the Great Depression. Ronald Reagan himself would vote for FDR all four times. Ronald Reagan put it well when he said, "I had become a Democrat, by birth, I suppose."[12] Reagan was here referring to his family's, especially his father's, identification with the Democratic Party throughout Reagan's early years. Once again, Jack and Nelle Reagan presented themselves as contrasting figures: Jack was a staunch Democrat, and Nelle, according to Neil Reagan, "just went along." The two sons, Neil and Ronald, followed their father and also counted themselves Democrats.[13] Jack's strong identification with the Democratic Party was unusual for rural Illinois, especially in Dixon, where most people were Republican. However, Jack felt strongly about racial and ethnic equality, and according to Ronald Reagan, he "was suspicious of established authority, especially the Republican politicians who ran the Illinois state government, which he considered as corrupt as Tammany Hall."[14] Jack Reagan did not have a sophisticated liberal ideology that he passed on to his sons. After all, the elder Reagan had only an elementary school education and rarely read any books on politics. However, from what he knew, Jack believed that the Democratic Party best represented his interests and values. This became particularly evident after the Great Depression hit in October 1929.

When the Great Depression struck, Ronald Reagan was attending Eureka College, and although it was financially difficult, he would continue at the college until graduation in 1932. However, Jack's dream of owning his own shoe store, which he had already named the Fashion Boot Shop, was lost shortly after the crash. Like millions of people across America, the Reagans endured financial hardship and looked forward to the 1932 presidential election. Their expectation was rewarded with Franklin Roosevelt's candidacy, and the Reagans responded to FDR with their support.

In the summer preceding the 1932 election, the effect of FDR's candidacy on the Reagans was palpable. Anne Edwards notes that "for the rest of the summer, Jack [Reagan] was caught up in Roosevelt's campaign, the chief topic of conversation at home. This was to be the first presidential election in which either Dutch [Ronald] or Moon [Neil] was to vote. Dutch cast his ballot for Roosevelt, . . . 'because I was a child of the Depression, a Democrat by upbringing and very emotionally involved.'"[15] Reagan recalls in his autobiography, "A few months after my twenty-first birthday, I cast my first vote for Roosevelt and the full Democratic ticket. And, like Jack—and millions of other Americans—I soon idolized FDR."[16]

And throughout his life, Ronald Reagan would continue to idolize FDR. Reagan's respect and admiration for FDR was based largely on FDR's personal leadership qualities. In his autobiography, Reagan observed that "during his Fireside Chats, [FDR's] strong, gentle, confident voice resonated across the nation with an eloquence that brought comfort and resilience to a nation caught up in a storm and reassured us that we could lick any problem. I will never forget him for that."[17] And of course FDR's New Deal would provide public employment to both Jack and Neil Reagan through the Federal Emergency Relief Administration (FERA). Both Jack and Neil received federal appointments to distribute federal funds in Lee County.[18] This New Deal patronage in exchange for the Reagan family's political support would also serve to strengthen Ronald Reagan's loyalty to FDR and the New Deal.

To Reagan, FDR was a true hero, and in many ways FDR became a lifelong role model for him. During the early years of the Depression, young Reagan was known to mimic FDR's speeches, utilizing a broom handle in place of a microphone. Later, Reagan would borrow FDR's expressions and phrases for speeches and would speak in glowing terms of FDR as a person and political leader. Decades later, this infuriated liberal critics of Reagan and confused his conservative supporters. How could Reagan express such admiration for a man who represented the antithesis of his conservative ideology?

The answer is largely found in Reagan's unique ability to separate FDR the person from FDR's New Deal policies and subsequent accretions—particularly the Great Society program of the 1960s. From his early adult years and continuing throughout his life, Reagan would admire and respect FDR's personal leadership qualities, including his communication skills and his decisive action during the Depression and war years. However, Reagan's understanding and evaluation of FDR's New Deal and its legacy would change over time.

Although Reagan considered himself a liberal Democrat during the 1930s and 1940s, his ideological understanding of liberalism was virtually nonexistent. As James David Barber noted in his profile of Reagan for his classic book *Presidential Character*, "After graduating from college [1932], Reagan got into radio as a sportscaster—a lucky choice, as broadcasting burgeoned during the Depression. Political ideology, if any, lay dormant in his life."[19] During his twenties and thirties, young Reagan was preoccupied with his career in sportscasting and his later acting career in Hollywood, he was preoccupied with his marriage to Jane Wyman in 1940 and then with starting a family, and he was preoccupied with his social life and the development of a variety of new friendships. These were his priorities. Little if any time was left over for any formal study of politics, especially any study about the differences between political conservatism and liberalism. Consequently, Reagan really held no political ideology from his youth through his early adult years. Not until his forties would he begin to think seriously about issues that would contribute toward a more coherent political philosophy.

Lou Cannon, a well-regarded Reagan biographer, argued along these same lines when he said that "Reagan is a cultural Democrat. And this is very, very important to understanding Reagan's success. His parents were Democrats. . . . Reagan did not pay much attention to Roosevelt's policies. He was grateful. He was not, as Garry Wills demonstrated in his book much better than I have in mine, a hemophiliac bleeding-heart liberal. He was a pretty orthodox follower of the New Deal. *He had very strong [core] values and not much of a political philosophy.*"[20]

So then how do we make sense of Reagan's journey when he lacked a political philosophy from the outset? Here, again, Barber demonstrates penetrating insight when he notes that "the course of Reagan's subsequent ideological development is much more clearly explained by the drift of his personal development than by any philosophical pilgrimage or burst of enlightenment."[21] Simply put, out of Ronald Reagan's personal experiences of the 1940s and 1950s, and not out of any philosophical or abstract enlightenment, would emerge Reagan's political philosophy and his identification with the Republican Party.

Many of Reagan's personal experiences during the 1930s and through the 1940s and 1950s were learning experiences about the value of American freedom. Reagan often described himself as a dreamer, and his early dreams of success—attending and graduating from college, becoming a sportscaster and then a Hollywood movie star—would not have been possible without freedom. Dreams, if they are to become reality, require freedom. Reagan therefore learned to value freedom not as an abstract concept but as something very tangible and real that had allowed him to improve his life. Peggy Noonan noted this in Reagan when she observed that "there was also the concrete and personal fact that he loved America because the freedom it offered gave him opportunity not only to enter adulthood on a firm footing but also to rescue his family during the Great Depression. It wasn't all abstract to him. And in later years he thought that he, without having tried to be, was living proof of the American dream."[22]

Reagan's journey from Democrat to Republican would commence with his perception that American freedom was threatened. To Reagan, American freedom was threatened by Communism and, as he would conclude later, by a growing and overly intrusive federal government. Reagan came to these conclusions largely through his own personal experiences. However, his conversations and debates with family members and friends, combined with his reading of various intellectuals, would assist him along a path that he had not anticipated. It was a path that would culminate in his registration with the Republican Party in 1962, when his journey from Democrat to Republican would be complete.

Notes

1. Ronald Reagan, *An American Life* (New York: Simon & Schuster, 1990), 22.
2. Ibid.
3. Lee Edwards, *Reagan: A Political Biography* (San Diego: Viewpoint, 1967), 12.
4. Ronald Reagan, *An American Life*, 22.
5. Ibid., emphasis added.
6. Ibid., 20–21.
7. Ibid., 27.
8. Ibid.
9. Ibid., 27–28.
10. Bill Boyarsky, *The Rise of Ronald Reagan* (New York: Random House, 1968), 28.
11. Ronald Reagan, *An American Life*, 28.
12. Ibid., 66.
13. Lee Edwards, *Reagan: A Political Biography*, 12.
14. Ronald Reagan, *An American Life*, 22.
15. Anne Edwards, *Early Reagan* (New York: William Morrow, 1987), 119.
16. Ronald Reagan, *An American Life*, 66.
17. Ibid.
18. Gary Wills, *Reagan's America* (New York: Doubleday, 1987), 61.
19. James David Barber, *The Presidential Character: Predicting Performance in the White House* (Englewood Cliffs, NJ: Prentice Hall, 1985), 473.
20. Eric Schmertz, Natalie Datlof, and Alexej Ugrinsky, eds., *Ronald Reagan's America* (Westport, CT: Greenwood Press, 1997), 2:714–15, emphasis added.
21. James David Barber, *The Presidential Character*, 472.
22. Peggy Noonan, *When Character Was King* (New York: Viking Press, 2001), 41–42.

CHAPTER TWO

~

The Communist Threat

In February 2001, the *Washington Post* observed, "Today, the concern about Soviet subversion that gripped the country through the late 1940s and 50s seems odd."[1] This *Post* observation provokes the obvious question: Why might Soviet subversion during the 1940s and 1950s appear odd to Americans a half century later? One plausible explanation is that the Cold War has now been over for more than ten years and the events of that conflict are increasingly remote to most Americans, especially the younger generation. Without historical grounding, Americans can fall prey to denying or minimizing the Communist threat to American freedom during those early years of the Cold War. Moreover, any mention today about Communist infiltration and subversion of American government and society during the late 1940s and through the 1950s is often categorically associated with the McCarthy hysteria of that period. That view, however, is a simplistic distortion of the historical record. Greater perspicuity is needed.

The Communist threat to infiltrate and subvert American society and institutions during the early Cold War years was real and palpable. Histories about this period are replete with evidence of Communist infiltration throughout American society, including the U.S. government. Some of the most compelling of this evidence has come after the collapse of the Soviet Union in 1991—evidence derived from researchers having unprecedented access to the archives of the Communist Party of the Soviet Union (CPSU). John Earl Haynes and Harvey Klehr have produced two books based on information obtained from the CPSU archives: *The Secret World of American*

Communism (1995) and *The Soviet World of American Communism* (1998). These books examine Soviet espionage efforts and the successful Communist infiltration of American society and government. The authors find evidence strongly linking the Communist Party of the United States (CPUSA) to the Communist Party of the Soviet Union. As expected, the two Communist organizations coordinated espionage activities against the U.S. government, labor unions, and other institutions of American society. Haynes and Klehr conclude that "until 1991 [and the collapse of the Soviet Union] American Communists, regardless of why they joined the CPUSA or what activities they engaged in as members, or even how aware they were of the fact, belonged to an organization [CPUSA] that was subservient to another [CPSU]."[2]

The release of the decoded Venona cables in 1995 further supports the claim that the CPSU and the CPUSA coordinated significant subversive espionage activities against the United States during the Cold War. In their book *Venona*, Haynes and Klehr have established CPSU and CPUSA success in penetrating American domestic targets, including the U.S. government. The authors note that "for more than forty years, nearly three thousand telegraphic cables between Soviet spies in the United States and their superiors in Moscow remained one of the United States government's most sensitive secrets."[3] With the help of the late Senator Daniel Patrick Moynihan of New York, several U.S. intelligence officials successfully argued for the official disclosure of the classified and decoded cables, collectively known as the Venona Project. The public ceremony announcing the official disclosure of the Venona Project occurred at CIA headquarters in Langley, Virginia, on July 11, 1995. After Haynes and Klehr read and digested the newly declassified decryptions, they concluded that the messages "fill in many gaps in the historical record and corroborate testimony from FBI files and congressional hearings. . . . The CPUSA was indeed a fifth column working inside and against the United States in the Cold War."[4] The scholarly controversy surrounding Communist infiltration, then, is actually over the degree of subversive activity, not whether it existed.

Within this milieu of Cold War activity, the entertainment industry assumed strategic significance for the Communists. Commenting about this period, Lou Cannon notes that "the Communist Party of the United States (CPUSA) accorded a high priority to Hollywood, then the citadel of American mass culture, during the two decades that Reagan made his principal living as a movie actor."[5] Cannon was merely noting the strategy of Lenin himself who once said, "Of all the arts, the cinema [for Communist propaganda] is the most important."[6] More specifically, however, Peter Schweizer states that "the Communist Party had been active in Hollywood since 1935, when a secret directive was issued by CPUSA (Communist Party of the U.S.A.) headquarters in New York calling for the capture of Hollywood's labor unions."[7] An earlier 1959 report by the Senate Fact Finding Committee on Un-American Activities of the California Legislature buttressed Schweizer's assessment with the charge that "the Communist Party working in Hollywood wanted control over everything that moved on wheels. . . . They soon moved Communist units into those unions having jurisdiction over carpenters, painters, musicians, grips and electricians. To control these trade unions was to control the motion picture industry."[8] But why would the Communists place such strategic importance on Hollywood? What would the Communists hope to gain? In his autobiography *An American Life*, Reagan explains that "American movies occupied seventy percent of all the playing time on the world's movie screens in those first years after World War II, and, as was to become more and more apparent (to me), Joseph Stalin had set out to make Hollywood an instrument of propaganda for his program of Soviet expansionism aimed at communizing the world."[9]

And yet as Reagan learned more about the Communist menace and its threat to American freedom, he would oppose Communist activity in Hollywood without the extremism of Joseph McCarthy. Reagan described his disagreement with McCarthy's tactics when he stated that McCarthy "was using a shotgun when he should have been using a rifle. . . . He went with a scatter gun and he lumped together fellow travelers, innocent dupes, and hard-core Communists."[10] Bill Boyarsky argues that "compared to some of his colleagues, [Reagan] was a moderate on the Communist issue."[11] Reagan pursued a middle course between two extremes demonstrated by many in Hollywood: On the one hand, some in Hollywood followed McCarthy's lead and made reckless allegations that injured innocent lives—these were often known as the red-baiters. On the other hand, others in Hollywood refused to cooperate with the U.S. government investigating Communist infiltration within the entertainment industry. As evidence of Reagan's moderation on the issue, Boyarsky notes that *Life* magazine was impressed with the testimony given by Reagan, Robert Montgomery, and George Murphy before the House Un-American Activities Committee. The magazine published that the three men "made their points neatly, with a good deal of restraint and common sense, and left the stand without dragging their feet."[12] Reagan's restraint was produced in large measure by his understanding that "if we get so frightened that we suspend our traditional democratic freedoms in order to fight them—they still have won. They [will] have shown that democracy won't work when the going gets tough."[13] Yes, Communist infiltration of

Hollywood during the 1940s and 1950s did occur, and it was opposed by Ronald Reagan through circumstances we are about to examine, but Reagan clearly differed from Joseph McCarthy in his opposition to Communism.

Nazi and Fascist Threats, but Communism?

At the end of World War II, Reagan knew very little about Communism. However, he was deeply opposed to Nazism and Fascism, which America and its allies had recently defeated. Reagan's disgust for the Nazis extended beyond their totalitarian ideology to his firsthand knowledge of their barbaric practices during the war. In fact, Nazi atrocities and war crimes left a deep and lifelong impression on Reagan, especially since he was one of the first Americans to discover direct visual evidence of Nazi war crimes.

Reagan had been assigned to Army Air Force Intelligence in Los Angeles, California, during the war in order to assist in making air force training films and documentaries. Reagan would often narrate films for pilots and their crew about to depart on bombing missions. He and others at the Hal Roach (Fort Roach) Film Studio in Culver City also prepared classified films about the progress of the war for staff in Washington, D.C. It was in this capacity that Reagan claims to have "handled a lot of classified footage taken by combat cameramen around the world that was never seen by the public."[14] This included classified film on Hitler's death camps. As Reagan himself recalled, "During the final months of the war, we began receiving secret Signal Corps films showing the liberation of Hitler's death camps and *they engraved images on my mind that will be there forever.*"[15]

This specific experience was combined with Reagan's general war experience and left him with a strong postwar revulsion to the vanquished Nazis and their palpable barbarism. However, Reagan was not convinced that the Nazi threat had been totally eliminated by the Allied victory over the Axis powers. Rather, after his return to civilian life, Reagan perceived the growing emergence of a Neo-Nazi or Neo-Fascist threat in the United States. Toward the end of 1945, Reagan felt that there were two growing and interrelated problems in the country that were largely ignored by the New Deal: Neo-Fascism and racial prejudice.[16] Reagan recalled that "old patterns of racism were reappearing after four years in which blacks and whites had fought side by side. My own industry, motion pictures, was being ripped apart by a bitter labor dispute. What troubled me most was what I saw as the rise of Fascism in our country, the very thing we had fought to obliterate. . . . Scores of new veterans' groups had sprouted up around the country and were trying to peddle some of the same venom of Fascist bigotry that we had just defeated in the war."[17]

While thinking about these issues, Reagan decided to take a more active role in opposing the threat to America. He joined a number of voluntary organizations, including the United World Federalists and the American Veterans Committee, in order to lend his voice to others in speaking out against "Fascist bigotry." And although Reagan recognized and responded to the threat of domestic Neo-Fascism at this time, he was largely ignorant of the threat to American liberty and values presented by Communism. After all, the Soviet Union had been our ally during the war, and according to Reagan, "he was not sharp about Communism and by reason of deception considered the American Communists in Hollywood liberals like himself."[18] In his book *Dutch*, Edmund Morris disputes the notion that Reagan was ignorant about Communism in the final months of 1945.[19] However, in his most recent autobiography, Reagan asserts, "When I'd come back to Warner Brothers after the war, I'd shared the orthodox liberal view that Communists—if there really *were* any—were liberals who were temporarily off track, and whatever they were, they didn't pose much of a threat to me or anyone. I heard whispers that Moscow wanted to infiltrate the world's most powerful medium of entertainment, but I'd passed them off as irrational and emotional red baiting. Now I knew from firsthand experience how Communists used lies, deceit, violence, or any other tactic that suited them to advance the cause of Soviet expansionism. I knew from the experience of hand-to-hand combat that America faced no more insidious or evil threat than that of Communism."[20] The key word Reagan used in describing how he became aware of the Communist threat was the word *tactic*. At this early stage in his experience with Communism, Reagan made no pretense to understanding fully the Communist ideology or to disputing its worldview, beliefs, and values. With time, however, Reagan grew more knowledgeable about Communist ideology and attacked its philosophy and its tactics. But at this early stage, Reagan's assessment of Communism was based largely upon the liberty-threatening tactics Communists employed to advance their cause. Communist tactics in Hollywood would arrest Reagan's attention and turn him into a formidable adversary of the Communist cause for the next forty years.

Communism in Hollywood

Reagan's growing awareness of the danger of Communism to liberty did not come primarily from reading and analysis. Rather, it came mostly from his *experience* in confronting Communist efforts and tactics to gain control of the motion picture industry in Hollywood. Within the time frame of 1945 to 1947, Reagan would encounter a rapid succession of mutually reinforcing experiences that would take him from a state of innocence about Communism to one of knowledge and militant opposition to the Communist threat. Although documenting each and every experience is beyond the scope of this book, three significant waves of experience can be identified clearly from 1945 to 1947 that shaped Reagan's views toward Communism.

The first wave of experience came immediately after World War II and was related to Reagan's desire to improve world conditions by joining a variety of voluntary organizations ostensibly set up for that purpose. Among the organizations selected by Reagan were the American Veterans Committee (AVC) and the Hollywood Independent Citizens Committee of the Arts, Sciences, and Professions (HICCASP). Even before being discharged from the military in August 1945, Reagan had "signed up as chairman of the AVC's Hollywood membership board."[21] In that capacity, he was "personally responsible for [recruiting] at least two hundred new members."[22] Reagan preferred the AVC to other veterans organizations because the AVC showed no evidence of bigotry and emphasized American citizenship over military service.[23] The organization's rather liberal constitution, which Reagan endorsed, among other provisions called for peaceful coexistence with the Soviet Union, cession of American nuclear power to the United Nations, full employment and a minimum wage, and comprehensive national health and education programs.[24] As Reagan participated in the AVC's activities throughout the early months of 1946, he grew increasingly aware of Communist activity within the organization. Edmund Morris notes that "not until April 26 [1946], when he attended the AVC's state convention in Los Angeles, did he notice with amazement that a tiny, well-organized minority of Communists manipulated the entire proceedings."[25] Because of his association with the AVC, Reagan was under surveillance by the FBI and was thought to be a Communist sympathizer.[26] However, a few months later, Reagan would experience other episodes revealing Communist tactics within the AVC that would lead to his resignation from the organization. Reagan recalled two of these incidents in which a Communist minority within the AVC utilized deceptive tactics to become a de facto majority in order to hold meetings and decide actions that otherwise would not have occurred due to their minority status.[27] Reagan called it an old Communist trick but new to him.[28] On another occasion, Reagan introduced a guest speaker at a luncheon conference and was embarrassed to "hear a recital of Stalinist tenets that were instantly adopted and passed."[29] After these episodes during the spring of 1946, Reagan states that he "resigned shortly thereafter from the AVC board and membership."[30] Morris states that "by June 14, when delegates [from the Hollywood AVC chapter] flew to Des Moines to attend the AVC's first national convention, the entire Los Angeles area council was under Communist control."[31]

Reagan's first wave of experience with Communism continued when he began to participate more fully during the summer and through the fall of 1946 in a second voluntary and ostensibly humanitarian organization—HIC-CASP—which would also disillusion Reagan and teach him more about Communist tactics.

Although Reagan had been a member of HICCASP since 1944,[32] he was not aware of Communist activity within the organization until after he became a member of its board of directors in June 1946.[33] With prominent members drawn from a variety of professions, including actress Olivia de Havilland, scientist Dr. Linus Pauling, and James Roosevelt (eldest son of the late president), HICCASP promoted a liberal agenda not unlike that promoted by the AVC, from which Reagan had resigned. Lou Cannon has described HICCASP as a "broad coalition of leftists and liberals supporting Franklin Roosevelt's fourth-term candidacy in 1944 [that] ended as a narrow Communist-controlled group that became the forerunner of the Independent Progressive Party, [and] nominated Henry Wallace for president in 1948."[34] Reagan's wake-up call to Communist activity within the organization came at his first board meeting on July 11, 1946.[35] In that meeting, Reagan once again experienced the animosity of Communists. A confrontation between Communists and non-Communists occurred when James Roosevelt called upon the board of directors to adopt a resolution condemning Fascism *and* Communism. Several Communist members were outraged and hurled personal insults at the United States and its government. Reagan supported the resolution and was rewarded with insults—he was called a Fascist, a witch hunter, and capitalist scum, though not necessarily in that order.[36] When Reagan was appointed to a seven-man committee to draft the resolution recommended by Roosevelt, he confronted further Communist tactics on the committee, resembling his experience with Communists within the AVC. Reagan was incredulous after he suggested that the "final statement, when approved, should go to all members of HICCASP for ratification and [John] Lawson snapped that the rank and file was not *politically intelligent enough* to vote on anything so fundamental as a set of principles."[37] Ultimately, the resolution faced heavy opposition and failed to pass. Numerous resignations then ensued, including the resignations of James Roosevelt and Olivia de Havilland. Reagan held on for a few months and then resigned shortly after October 1946.[38]

And so, within a matter of months during 1946, Reagan became very disappointed, and his hopes for world rehabilitation through the AVC and HICCASP were dashed. He had learned something about Communist infiltration and tactics that had forced him to resign from both organizations. Reagan would remember the undemocratic tactics employed in both organizations, particularly Communist efforts to disenfranchise majority rule combined with a disdain for the "rank and file." But as this first wave of experience with Communism was about to end, a second wave of experience would enlarge and reinforce Reagan's nascent views toward Communism even further.

This second wave of experience with Communists in Hollywood occurred while Reagan was a member of the board of directors of the Screen Actors Guild (SAG) during the fall of 1946. Founded in 1933, the Screen Actors Guild was the union organization representing actors and actresses in Hollywood. With the assistance of Jane Wyman, who would become Reagan's first wife in 1940, Reagan became a member of the board of directors not long after he arrived in Hollywood. Reagan stated, "In 1938, a novice in Hollywood, I suddenly found myself on the board of the SAG. The reason for it was not my fame nor fortune nor talents—but simply that the board had created a policy of a broad representation of all segments of the actors' world. . . . One of the vacancies happened to fit my classification: new, young contract player. I accepted with awe and pleasure."[39] Reagan remained on the board until his enlistment into the army during World War II, but as soon as he returned to civilian life in 1945, he received a reappointment. Reagan describes these events in his first autobiography when he observes, "I had to resign from the board when I was swept into the Army but I kept in touch. Almost as soon as I got out in 1945, I was reappointed to the board and found myself swept into a maelstrom of the most rugged decisions I have ever had to make."[40]

Most of these "rugged decisions" were linked to an alleged Communist-inspired labor dispute that involved the SAG and other unions in Hollywood. By the fall of 1946, Herb Sorrell, head of the Conference of Studio Unions (CSU), called for a jurisdictional strike in order to expand the CSU's influence and control in Hollywood. In his book *Reagan's War*, Peter Schweizer argues that Sorrell had links to the Communist Party and Communist Party front organizations, and "if Sorrell succeeded, the Communists believed, they could run Hollywood."[41] Sorrell and the CSU were prepared for and incited violence during the strike, which ran from September of 1946 through February of 1947. CSU strikers "smashed windshields on passing trains and threw rocks at the police. One studio employee went to the hospital after acid was thrown in his face."[42] The same threat was directed at Reagan as well. On September 24, while he was working on the movie *Night unto Night*, Reagan received a telephone call, and as he later recalled, the caller wouldn't identify himself but threatened to disfigure Reagan's face with acid if he continued to oppose the CSU and its strike agenda in Hollywood.[43]

Reagan had assumed an important role investigating the CSU strike and was preparing to deliver a speech to the SAG membership recommending that the SAG not recognize the strike but rather cross the CSU picket line. Reagan was convinced that the telephone threat was from the CSU, but at that time he may not have made the link between the CSU and Communist subversion.[44] In any case, Reagan took the threat seriously and reported it to the director of the picture. Shortly thereafter, Blaney Matthews, the security head at Warner Brothers, made sure that Reagan got a permit to carry a .32 Smith & Wesson pistol for protection.[45] Reagan placed the gun in a holster and wore it under his jacket during waking hours, and when he went to sleep, he kept it at his bedside.[46] He carried the pistol for the next seven months[47] and hired guards to protect his children.[48] This was obviously a stressful time for Ronald Reagan and his family. However, the stress did not stop there. Peter Schweizer observes that "along with the threats of physical violence, Communist Party members in the industry began verbally attacking Reagan and others for their stand [in opposing the CSU strike]."[49] Actor Alexander Knox called Reagan a "fraud," actress Karen Morley called him an opportunist, and the CSU called for a boycott of his movies.[50] Reagan, however, remained firm and effectively opposed the strike. Several years later, Reagan's strike actions were complimented by actor Sterling Hayden in testimony before the House Committee on Un-American Activities. In a committee hearing, Hayden testified about his participation in various Communist strategies to influence Hollywood, and when asked why the Communist strategies had failed, Hayden answered, "We ran into the Board of Directors of the SAG and particularly into Ronald Reagan, who was a one-man battalion."[51] Reagan would take great pride in this description, later referring to it as "one of the best reviews I ever got."[52] His actions during the strike were also recognized and praised by movie producer Jack Warner, who proclaimed that "Ronnie Reagan . . . has turned out to be a tower of strength."[53] Others complimented Reagan as well.[54] Thus, Reagan increasingly became a polarizing figure in Hollywood at the time of the CSU strike: Some people deeply despised him, yet others respected and supported him. This fact had become increasingly obvious to Reagan over the course of the strike, but its stark reality was impressed on him even further when the FBI visited him at his home. Reagan recalls that "one night just before bedtime, during the strike, there was a knock at my front door. I peeked through a little hole in the door and saw two men holding up the credentials of FBI agents."[55] Reagan invited the agents in, and they asked him if he would cooperate in providing information about Communist activities in Hollywood. An agent informed Reagan that "anybody that the Communists hate as much as they do you must know something that can help us."[56] Moreover, the FBI told Reagan that his name had come up during a meeting of the American Communist Party in downtown Los Angeles a few nights earlier in which one of the Party members had said, "What the hell are we going to do about that son-of-a-bitching bastard Reagan?"[57] This report confirmed what Reagan had come to understand within the relatively short period of a few months in 1946: He was hated by Communist Party members, including colleagues and former friends in Hollywood. He agreed to cooperate with the FBI by providing periodic reports about Communist activities in Hollywood. Garry Wills argues that this meeting may have been important in convincing Reagan that the CSU strike was Communist inspired. Wills argues, "It was from this period, if not from this session, that Reagan hardened forever his belief that the CSU strike was part of a Communist plot."[58] Whether the Communists were actually behind the CSU strike has been the subject of some debate. However, in both of his autobiographies, Reagan has consistently cited the California Senate Fact Finding Reports on Un-American Activities to support his claim that Communists were behind the CSU strike.

By the end of the CSU strike in February of 1947, Reagan was a transformed man. He self-admittedly had left the military in 1945 with an ignorant and naive view of Communism. His experiences during 1946 changed much of that. Within a single year, he had encountered Communist tactics and hostility in two voluntary organizations, leading to his resignations from both, and Communist sponsorship of an illegitimate strike that included violence to many in Hollywood and violent threats against Reagan himself. These experiences contributed significantly to Reagan's growing realization that Communism represented as great a threat to American freedom as Fascism had just a few years earlier. In his book *Dutch*, Morris recognized the importance of Reagan's experiences in 1946 when he observed that "in '46 both the AVC and HICCASP went pink on him. Then in the fall the labor situation in Hollywood broke down again. Things got really ugly, and Reagan became a red-baiter almost overnight."[59] However, Reagan would continue to learn about his Communist adversary and its threat to American freedom in the years ahead. Most immediately, however, the third wave of his experience with Communism would evolve from his decision to accept the presidency of the Screen Actors Guild in 1947. Reagan would once again experience and confront Communist subversive activity in Hollywood, but this last wave of experience would largely serve to reinforce and confirm the anti-Communist views he had developed in 1946. From a position of significant influence as president of the Screen Actors Guild, representing approximately 15,000 Hollywood employees, Reagan would continue his battle against Communism.

He ascended to the presidency of the Screen Actors Guild shortly after the CSU strike ended in February 1947. The following month, Reagan and his wife, Jane Wyman, attended a regular meeting of the SAG board of directors. Surprisingly, seven members submitted their resignations that evening, including the president of the guild, Robert Montgomery. Montgomery, who had been recently elected to the position, was "weary of the political battles that were erupting . . . and very much concerned about retribution against anti-Communists in Hollywood."[60] Gene Kelly therefore nominated Reagan to replace Montgomery, and Reagan won the election against two other candidates. Reagan's views toward Communism had hardened considerably by this time. In his autobiography An American Life, Reagan states that "the strike and the efforts to gain control over HICCASP and other organizations had a profound effect on me. More than anything else, it was the Communists' attempted takeover of Hollywood and its worldwide weekly audience of more than five hundred million people that led me to accept a nomination to serve as president of the Screen Actors Guild and, indirectly at least, set me on the road that would lead me into politics."[61] Upon accepting the nomination and getting elected to the presidency of the SAG, Reagan knew quite well that his fight with the Communists would continue, but he may not have known the extent of the threat within the SAG itself. However, in his book Reagan's War, Peter Schweizer argues that upon assuming the presidency of the SAG, Reagan "quickly discovered that two small cliques made up of Communist Party members were active in the SAG leadership. The strike had radicalized them and they were now posing a serious challenge."[62] The factions were led by two women, Karen Morley and Anne Revere, who were indeed party members.[63] Reagan was less concerned with their political philosophy than with their tactics in advancing Communist influence within the guild. He was especially concerned that a Communist secret agenda might supercede the interests of the SAG. Consequently, Reagan proposed a resolution later in the year that "no Communist Party member could be an officer of the Guild."[64] The resolution passed the SAG membership 1,307 to 157, though Morley and Revere intensely opposed it.[65] Reagan would continue to oppose Communist activity within the guild throughout his six terms as president of the union.

As president of the SAG, Reagan would also continue consulting with the FBI. He lost no time in meeting the FBI just one month after his election to discuss Communist influence within the guild. At that April 10, 1947, meeting, Reagan and his wife informed the FBI that "there were two cliques of members, one headed by Anne Revere and the other by Karen Morley which on all questions of policy confronting the Guild, followed the Communist Party line."[66] Reagan also agreed at this meeting to periodically report to the FBI the "names of any members of the SAG who he thought had Communist associations."[67] According to Garry Wills, Reagan and his wife "named at least six people at the April 10th meeting, one of whom led the support for Sorrell's [CSU] strike within the membership, and others of whom belonged to one of two cliques that follow the Communist Party line."[68] Reagan met with the FBI frequently enough to be given the informer's code number: T-10.[69]

Reagan also cooperated with other elements of the federal government investigating Communism in Hollywood, most notably the House Committee on Un-American Activities convened in October 1947. Reagan had received a subpoena a month earlier to appear before the committee and testify, along with many actors, directors, and writers. The committee was specifically interested in learning more about Communist activity in Hollywood, and the president of the SAG would provide important testimony toward that end. The hearings began on October 20, 1947, and five days later Reagan delivered his testimony to the committee, following the testimony provided that same day by George Murphy and former SAG president Robert Montgomery. Reagan was questioned by the chief investigator for the committee, Robert Stripling. Reagan revealed what he had learned about Communism in an exchange with Stripling. That exchange included the following excerpts:[70]

> STRIPLING: As a member of the board of directors, as president of the Screen Actors Guild, and as an active member, have you at any time observed or noted within the organization a clique of either Communists or Fascists who were attempting to exert influence or pressure on the guild?
> REAGAN: Well, sir, my testimony must be very similar to that of Mr. Murphy and Mr. Montgomery. There has been a small group within the Screen Actors Guild which has consistently opposed the policy of the guild board and officers of the guild, as evidenced by the vote on various issues. That small clique referred to has been suspected of more or less following the tactics that we associate with the Communist Party.
> STRIPLING: Would you refer to them as a disruptive influence within the guild?
> REAGAN: I would say that at times they have attempted to be a disruptive influence.

And in later testimony, Reagan would once again refer to Communist tactics:

STRIPLING: Would you say from your observation that that is typical of the tactics or strategy of the Communists, to solicit and use the names of prominent people to either raise money or gain support?

REAGAN: I think it is in keeping with their tactics; yes, sir.

STRIPLING: Do you think there is anything democratic about those tactics?

REAGAN: I do not, sir.

And finally Reagan would refer to Communist tactics in his concluding statement:

REAGAN: Sir, if I might, in regard to that, say that what I was trying to express, and didn't do very well, was also this other fear. I detest, I abhor their [the Communists] philosophy, but I detest more than that their tactics, which are those of the fifth column, and are dishonest, but at the same time I never as a citizen want to see our country become urged, by either fear or resentment of this group, that we ever compromise with any of our democratic principles through that fear or resentment. I still think that democracy can do it.

CHAIRMAN [of the committee] J. PARNELL THOMAS: We agree with that. Thank you very much.

What Reagan Learned about the Communist Threat

Within the relatively brief time frame of 1945 to 1947, Ronald Reagan progressed from being self-admittedly naive and unsophisticated about Communism to being a formidable adversary. Reagan learned during this period that Communism was a real and palpable threat to American freedom. He came to this conclusion largely through his direct experience with Communist infiltration activities in Hollywood during the first two years after World War II. Reagan learned of the Communist threat in three successive waves of experience. And although this did not account for all of Reagan's experience with the Communist threat, the three waves of experience discussed in this chapter were major episodes of highly compressed and reinforcing experiences that transformed Reagan's thinking about Communism. His views about Communism by 1947 would remain largely unaltered throughout his subsequent political career, including his presidency. And so an important question is, What did Reagan learn about the Communist threat to freedom during this time frame? Although we cannot undertake a comprehensive assessment of what Reagan learned, we can identify four major lessons Reagan learned during the early stages of his journey from Democrat to Republican.

First, out of his experience with extremist ideologies such as Nazism, Fascism, and Communism, Reagan discarded the notion of an ideological continuum and instead lumped the ideologies all together as totalitarian threats to freedom. The extremist ideologies resembled one another by advocating the rule of the few over the many. To Reagan, this elitist rule, whether from the right or the left, was tantamount to tyranny and threatened the people's freedom. Reagan had reached this conclusion by May of 1947, when he argued that "our highest aim should be the cultivation of freedom of the individual, for therein lies the highest dignity of man. Tyranny is tyranny and—whether it comes from the Right, Left or Center—it is evil. I suspect the extreme right and the extreme left of political ideologies, though seeming to branch off in opposite directions, curve to a common meeting point."[71] Reagan further defined the nature of the threat just a few years later in a January 1951 article published in *Fortnight*. He argued that "the real fight with this new totalitarianism [Communism] belongs properly to the forces of liberal democracy, just as did the battle with Hitler's totalitarianism. There really is no difference except in the cast of characters. On one hand is our belief that the people can and will decide what is best for themselves, and on the other [Communist, Nazi, or Fascist] side is the belief that a *few* can best decide what is good for all the rest."[72]

On numerous occasions, Reagan's experience with extremist ideologies taught him that they were defined largely in terms of the few ruling or attempting to rule the many. His understanding of Communism in particular developed during his time with voluntary associations, during the SAG strike, and during his tenure as president of the SAG when he experienced numerous occasions in which a small minority of Communist Party members attempted to impose their agenda on an unsuspecting majority often held in contempt by the Communists. Reagan spoke about their strategy when he observed, "We know how the Communists have sought to infiltrate and control certain key industries. We know they operate with a 1 percent minority but depend on organization. At meetings they come early and stay late and they get confused liberals to front for them at all times."[73] Another example of this was cited in Reagan's first autobiography in which he recalled his interest in submitting an issue to the entire membership of HICCASP for a vote, only to encounter opposition by radical and suspected Communist John Lawson, who replied, "The membership isn't politically sophisticated enough to make this decision."[74] To Reagan, this statement captured the right, left, or center totalitarian mind-set. Reagan stated, "It was the first time I had ever heard the phrase. It was a goodie. I still hear it used and like Pavlov's dog I react, particularly when innocents use it defending the idea of government by an intellectual elite."[75] Future political statements that would refer to the American people as the "masses" and that supported elite rule by experts would naturally arouse Reagan's suspicion since in his mind they so closely resembled the common basis of totalitarian ideologies.

A second important lesson Reagan learned about Communism during this postwar period was that Communist tactics were more dangerous than its philosophy—and Communist tactics needed to be confronted and defeated. This lesson was apparent in Reagan's congressional testimony in 1947. In this vein, Schweizer observes, "The threat posed by Communism, as [Reagan] had said in his Congressional testimony, was not so much its ideas but its tactics. In a straight ideological battle between freedom and Communism, he was confident freedom would always come out on top. The problem was that Communists masked their agenda and had fooled some otherwise loyal Americans into believing that the Communist Party sought to make a better world."[76] Reagan's proclivity toward emphasizing the fight against Communist tactics rather than its philosophy was clearly demonstrated in his article "How Do You Fight Communism?" published in *Fortnight* in January 1951. In the article, Reagan emphasized the danger of various Communist tactics and recommended counterstrategies to oppose the Communists. Reagan's primary argument was that the threat of international Communism was truly and quite simply Russian nationalistic aggression. To oppose the Communists effectively, Reagan argued, "Suppose we quit using the words Communist and Communism? They are a hoax perpetrated by the Russian Government, to aid in securing fifth columnists [infiltrators] in other countries and to mask Russian aggression aimed at world conquest. Every time we make the issue one of Communism as a political philosophy we help in this hoax. Substitute 'Pro-Russian' for the word Communist and watch the confusion disappear. Then you can say to any American, 'You are free to believe any political theory (including Communism) you want,' but the so-called Communist Party is nothing more or less than a 'Russian-American Bund' owing allegiance to Russia and supporting Russia in its plan to conquer the world."[77] Nine years later, in a letter explaining his political views to Hugh Hefner, Reagan disclosed that his position on this issue had not changed. Reagan wrote, "I, like you, will defend the right of any American to openly practice & preach any political philosophy from monarchy to anarchy. But this is not the case with regard to the Communist. He is bound by party discipline to deny that he is a Communist so that he can by subversion and stealth impose on an unwilling people the rule of the International Communist Party, which is in fact the govt. of Soviet Russia."[78]

Although there is no evidence that Reagan had systematically studied Marxist-Leninist ideology during the late 1940s and early 1950s, he sensed the weakness in Communist doctrine and felt the true battle with Communism was a tactical one. This approach, too, appealed to Reagan's value of practical experience over intellectual abstractions, and of course Reagan had plenty of practical experience in dealing with Communist tactics. Schweizer captures this dimension of Reagan's approach to Communism and contrasts it quite effectively with Joe McCarthy's. Schweizer writes, "What separated Reagan from McCarthy and some of the other anti-Communists at the time was his belief in the profound weakness of Communism. For McCarthy, the ideology was a thing to be feared, an ironclad doctrine with strong adherents. For Reagan, on the other hand, Communism appealed to the weak. Far from being a sign of intellectual strength or political courage, its wellspring was personal weakness. . . . It wasn't that Reagan was minimizing the threat; he believed that Communism was a profound challenge. But he believed it thrived only by secrecy, threats, and deceit."[79] Because Reagan focused on opposing Communist tactics rather than ideology, in contrast to McCarthy who emphasized a fight against Communist ideology, Reagan's opposition to Communism was more moderated than McCarthy's. Reagan was chiefly concerned with exposing and defeating secretive, deceptive, and nondemocratic Communist practices; he was not preoccupied with eradicating Communist ideology from the public square. However, because McCarthy was much more threatened by Communist ideology, his actions in opposing Communists were often extreme and violated the very civil liberties our democratic government was established to protect.

This led to Reagan's third lesson derived from his experiences during the early postwar years: The protection of American democratic values must be maintained and cannot be abdicated in the fight against Communism. In other words, Reagan came to the conclusion that America could not fight the Communists with the same deceptive and nondemocratic tactics employed by the Communists against America. As Dinesh D'Souza observes, "Reagan saw firsthand that they [Communists] were not inhibited by traditional moral constraints and were willing to practice deceit and even violence to further their ideological cause. *Reagan, however, refused to use the same tactics in opposing the Communists.*"[80] Reagan criticized Joseph McCarthy for his anti-Communist tactics, which often injured the innocent, and Reagan affirmed in his 1947 Congressional testimony that in dealing with Communism, "I never as a citizen want to see our country . . . compromise with any of our democratic principles."[81] In practice, Reagan's actions were consistent with his words. In his 1947 congressional testimony, he opposed federal legislation that would make it a crime to espouse Communist beliefs or belong to the Communist Party, and he defended the rights of SAG members who were wrongly accused of Communist affiliations.[82] He clearly opposed the Communists, but he was not willing to sacrifice American values and principles in the process. A few years after his 1947 congressional testimony, Reagan still articulated the same message in an article for *Fortnight* magazine. Reagan once again argued that "if we get so frightened that we suspend our traditional democratic freedoms in order to fight them—they still have won. They have shown then that Democracy won't work when the going gets tough."[83] Overall, Reagan pursued a middle course in his reaction to Communism. On the one hand, he did not resist investigative efforts by the federal government (as some in Hollywood did), since he did cooperate with the FBI and the House Committee on Un-American Activities investigating Communist activity in Hollywood. On the other hand, Reagan's approach in opposing the Communist threat was significantly more restrained than many in both Hollywood and Washington at the time.

Though Reagan was cognizant about the danger of sacrificing civil liberties and undermining American values in the fight against Communism, he still pursued a circumscribed fight because he was convinced of the Communist menace and its threat to American freedom. However, many in Hollywood and elsewhere, though not Communist, refused to cooperate with federal investigations and were reluctant to oppose the Communists since they saw the Communists as presenting little or no threat to the United States. Many of these people considered themselves liberals, and of course Reagan had identified with them before his postwar experiences with Communism.

However, after his three waves of experience with Communists, Reagan learned his fourth lesson: American liberalism is vulnerable to deception and manipulation by the Communists. Largely because of his experience with Communism in the early postwar years, Reagan learned that the Communist was fundamentally *different* from the liberal. Reagan was convinced that most liberals were deceived about Communists. To Reagan, liberal beliefs and values made it difficult to (1) distinguish the Communist from the liberal and (2) appreciate the real threat posed by the Communists to American freedom. In short, Reagan came to believe that liberals were not treasonous but rather were dangerously naive and were deceived about Communism. In his first autobiography, Reagan stated that his revised views about liberalism were taking shape just as his views about Communism were being developed. Shortly after he resigned from HICCASP in 1946, Reagan recalled that "light was dawning in some obscure region in my head. I was beginning to see the seamy side of liberalism. Too many of the patches on the progressive coat were of a color I didn't personally care for. Something the liberal will have to explain and stand trial for is his inability to see the Communist as he truly is and not as some kind of Peck's Bad Boy of liberalism who is basically all right but just a bit overboard and rough-edged. This ideological myopia is even true of some who have met the Reds in philosophical combat and who should have learned something from crossing swords."[84] Later, in his second autobiography and after his presidency, Reagan would write that "I was to discover that a lot of liberals just couldn't accept the notion that Moscow had bad intentions or wanted to take over Hollywood and many other American industries through subversion, or that Stalin was a murderous gangster. To them, fighting totalitarianism was 'witchhunting' and 'red baiting.'"[85] Reagan was careful not to call liberals pro-Communist, but he did refer to them as anti-anti-Communists. In other words, liberals foolishly opposed those who were opposed to the Communists. To Reagan, liberals were deceived about the Communists, and their deception and vulnerability to Communist manipulation was dangerous to the nation. Liberals must see the light as Reagan had seen the light, and so Reagan saw a patriotic obligation to inform and educate "liberal-thinking Americans [who had] not joined in the anti-Communist contest."[86] Reagan would therefore use his influential position as president of the SGA to speak out against the Communist threat.

In 1948, Reagan acted upon his more hardened anti-Communist views by supporting Harry Truman's candidacy for reelection rather than Henry Wallace's bid, which many liberal Democrats supported. Truman articulated a more confrontational policy to the Soviets than the more conciliatory approach preferred by Wallace. Just four years later, Reagan would vote Republican for the first time. His vote was cast for Republican presidential candidate Dwight Eisenhower. In the race between Eisenhower and Democratic nominee Stevenson, Eisenhower articulated a bolder position of rolling back Communism rather than simply containing it as proposed by Stevenson and the Democrats. Reagan's newly developed views about Communism supported Eisenhower's position, though after Eisenhower's election a divergence between Eisenhower's rhetoric and practice on the issue would disappoint Reagan. Gradual yet palpable changes were developing in Reagan's political evolution. Although Reagan remained a Democrat during the 1950s, he voted for Ike in both presidential elections.

During the 1950s, Reagan would detect and confront another growing threat to American freedom. In contrast to the Communist threat, this threat would find its nucleus in the growing U.S. federal bureaucracy of the 1950s and 1960s. And, although not a foreign menace to freedom, the growing federal bureaucracy would, in Reagan's view, still pose a threat to American freedom. After all, Reagan would remember the lessons he had learned about Communism earlier and observe the ominous emergence of elite rule by Washington bureaucrats. This second threat would have to be exposed and confronted as well. Reagan would undertake the task, but it would come more gradually than Reagan's earlier response to the threat of Communism. Reagan's employment with General Electric from 1954 to 1962 would provide the fundamental experience for his learning about and reacting to this second threat to American freedom.

Notes

1. John Meroney, "Rehearsals for a Lead Role: Ronald Reagan Was a Liberal, an Actor, a Labor Chief—but Some Unscripted Plot Twists Forged a New Character," *Washington Post*, February 4, 2001, Final Edition, Sunday Arts Section, G01.

2. Harvey Klehr, John Earl Haynes, and Kyrill M. Anderson, *The Soviet World of American Communism* (New Haven, CT: Yale University Press, 1998), 8.

3. John Earl Haynes and Harvey Klehr, *Venona* (New Haven, CT: Yale University Press, 1999), 1.

4. Ibid., 7.

5. Lou Cannon, *President Reagan: The Role of a Lifetime* (New York: Simon & Schuster, 1991), 283.

6. Peter Schweizer, *Reagan's War* (New York: Doubleday, 2002), 7.

7. Ibid.

8. Lee Edwards, *Reagan: A Political Biography* (San Diego: Viewpoint, 1967), 53.

9. Ronald Reagan, *An American Life* (New York: Simon & Schuster, 1990), 110.

10. Peter Schweizer, *Reagan's War*, 19–20.

11. Bill Boyarsky, *The Rise of Ronald Reagan* (New York: Random House, 1968), 89.

12. Ibid., 91.

13. Peter Schweizer, *Reagan's War*, 19.

14. Ronald Reagan, *An American Life*, 99.

15. Ibid., emphasis added.

16. Edmund Morris, *Dutch* (New York: Random House, 1999), 227.

17. Ronald Reagan, *An American Life*, 105–6.

18. Anne Edwards, *Early Reagan* (New York: William Morrow, 1987), 300.

19. Edmund Morris, *Dutch*, 227.

20. Ronald Reagan, *An American Life*, 115.

21. Edmund Morris, *Dutch*, 221.

22. Ibid., 222.

23. Ronald Reagan and Richard Hubler, *Where's the Rest of Me?* (New York: Dell, 1965), 189–90.

24. Edmund Morris, *Dutch*, 229.

25. Ibid., 230.

26. Garry Wills, *Reagan's America* (New York: Doubleday, 1987), 246.

27. Ronald Reagan and Richard Hubler, *Where's the Rest of Me?* 189–90.

28. Ibid.

29. Edmund Morris, *Dutch*, 231.

30. Ronald Reagan and Richard Hubler, *Where's the Rest of Me?* 190.

31. Edmund Morris, *Dutch*, 231.

32. Peter Schweizer, *Reagan's War*, 9.

33. Anne Edwards, *Early Reagan*, 302.

34. Lou Cannon, *President Reagan: The Role of a Lifetime*, 284.

35. Anne Edwards, *Early Reagan*, 302.

36. Edmund Morris, *Dutch*, 233.

37. Ibid., 233–34, emphasis added.

38. Ibid., 234.

39. Ronald Reagan and Richard Hubler, *Where's the Rest of Me?* 153.

40. Ibid., 154.

41. Peter Schweizer, *Reagan's War*, 6.

42. Ibid., 10.

43. Ronald Reagan, *An American Life*, 108.

44. Peggy Noonan, *When Character Was King* (New York: Viking Press, 2001), 57.

45. Peter Schweizer, *Reagan's War*, 12.

46. Ibid.

47. Peggy Noonan, *When Character Was King*, 56–57.

48. Peter Schweizer, *Reagan's War*, 11–12.

49. Ibid., 12.

50. Ibid.

51. Lee Edwards, *Reagan: A Political Biography*, 54.

52. Ronald Reagan, *An American Life*, 114.

53. Peter Schweizer, *Reagan's War*, 12.

54. Ibid.

55. Ronald Reagan, *An American Life*, 111.

56. Ibid.

57. Ibid.

58. Garry Wills, *Reagan's America*, 247.

59. Edmund Morris, *Dutch*, 237.

60. Peter Schweizer, *Reagan's War*, 13.

61. Ronald Reagan, *An American Life*, 114.

62. Peter Schweizer, *Reagan's War*, 13.

63. Ibid., 14.

64. Ibid.

65. Ibid.

66. Ibid.

67. Anne Edwards, *Early Reagan*, 322.

68. Garry Wills, *Reagan's America*, 249.

69. Ibid.

70. Anne Edwards, *Early Reagan*, 344–49.

71. Lee Edwards, *Reagan: A Political Biography*, 58.

72. Ronald Reagan, "How Do You Fight Communism?" *Fortnight*, January 22, 1951, 13.

73. Ibid.

74. Ronald Reagan and Richard Hubler, *Where's the Rest of Me?* 193.

75. Ibid.

76. Peter Schweizer, *Reagan's War*, 19.

77. Ronald Reagan, "How Do You Fight Communism?" *Fortnight*, 13.

78. Edmund Morris, *Dutch*, 236.

79. Peter Schweizer, *Reagan's War*, 20.

80. Dinesh D'Souza, *Ronald Reagan: How an Ordinary Man Became an Extraordinary Leader* (New York: Free Press, 1997), 48, emphasis added.

81. Ibid.

82. Ibid.

83. Ronald Reagan, "How Do You Fight Communism?" *Fortnight*, 13.

84. Ronald Reagan and Richard Hubler, *Where's the Rest of Me?* 194.

85. Ronald Reagan, *An American Life*, 110.

86. Ronald Reagan, "How Do You Fight Communism?" *Fortnight*, 13.

CHAPTER THREE

~

The "Encroaching" Federal Government

Ronald Reagan's understanding about the Communist threat to American freedom developed earlier and more rapidly than his perception that a growing federal government posed a threat to American freedom as well. Reagan's learning was sequential. His three waves of experience with Communism discussed in chapter 2 occurred over a relatively brief time period (1945 to 1947) and led to views about opposing Communism that remained largely unaltered throughout his life. On the other hand, Reagan's distrustful views about an activist federal government, although beginning to develop during the Great Depression and throughout the early postwar years, emerged coherently by the end of the 1950s. His employment with General Electric (GE) was particularly influential, since it provided experiences that would shape his domestic policy views for the rest of his life. In fact, the GE years would contribute significantly to a coherent political philosophy for Reagan, which would include a diminished role for the federal government and an expanded one for American business. As Lou Cannon noted, "More than anything, it is his GE experience that changed Reagan from an adversary of big business into one of its most ardent spokesmen."[1]

However, Reagan still considered himself a New Deal liberal prior to his employment with GE. This meant that he held a generally suspicious and distrustful view of business, especially big business, and a more positive view of FDR's New Deal and the federal government's expanded role in the economy. Remember, Reagan had been raised in a family with close ties to the Democratic Party and special loyalty to the "working man" and Franklin

Roosevelt's New Deal program. In his second autobiography, Reagan observed, "As a liberal in my younger days I'd had an inherent suspicion of big business."[2] Peggy Noonan also notes that for Reagan, "all his life he'd shared his father's skepticism about big companies; he was skeptical of great power centers that had the ability to push people around and abuse workers."[3] Reagan's distrust of American business would undergo a major transformation during his period of employment with GE. By the end of the 1950s, he would come to greatly appreciate the industry, innovation, and wealth-creating attributes of American business. On the other hand, Reagan's views toward the federal government were altered by a number of earlier experiences stretching back to the early 1930s. These personal experiences combined to induce a set of grievances against the federal government even before Reagan accepted the GE offer to host *General Electric Theater*.

For instance, as early as 1933, when he was only twenty-two years old, young Reagan, observing his father's work with the federal government, concluded that dysfunctional governmental incentives made it difficult for the unemployed to effectively make the transition from welfare to work. Reagan concluded from the experience that the "wheels were turning in Washington and government was busy at the job it does best—growing."[4] The experience was an important one, and as Reagan biographer Lee Edwards notes, "It was Ronald Reagan's first close look at the ways of the federal government and it made a lasting impression."[5] There were other reinforcing experiences as well.

A little more than ten years later, toward the end of World War II, Captain Reagan learned something about the civilian bureaucracy at Fort Roach that created, in his words, "the first crack in my staunch liberalism."[6] It appears that here, too, Reagan came in contact with the government's propensity to grow. In his first autobiography, Reagan recounts that the personnel office responsible for his new civilian section of 250 people was twice the size of the personnel section responsible for the records of 1,300 military officers and men. Reagan recalls that "their (civilian) rules and regulations filled shelves from floor to ceiling, around virtually the four walls of a barrack-sized building."[7] Moreover, Reagan experienced considerable difficulty in removing an incompetent secretary from her civilian position. The person in charge of civilian personnel informed Reagan that, short of a trial, the incompetent secretary would be moved to another assignment—actually, an improved assignment. This remedy suggested an intrinsic dysfunction within the bureaucracy for Reagan. He concluded that the secretary "could be moved to another assignment, even though doing so meant an improved assignment. So the incompetent wound up with a promotion and a raise in pay.

No one in the administrative hierarchy of civil service will ever interfere with this upgrading process because his own pay and rating are based on the number of employees beneath him and the grades of those employees. *It's a built-in process for empire-building.*"[8] And so, early on, well before Reagan's employment with GE, he had begun to identify dysfunctions, particularly the federal government's propensity to grow, even though he considered himself a New Deal liberal. Reinforcing experiences would continue during Reagan's post–World War II years in Hollywood.

Only a few years after the war, while Reagan was president of the Screen Actors Guild, the federal government launched an antitrust action in 1948 that effectively split theater ownership away from the major movie producers. Reagan believed the federal action to be terribly misguided, unjust, and damaging to the movie industry. In his first autobiography, Reagan argued that the action contributed "to the final disintegration of Hollywood as the key movie manufacturer of the world."[9] Reagan continued to hold strong views against the federal antitrust action even after his presidency. In his second autobiography, written after his presidency, Reagan argued, "I believe the government's decision to break up the studio system was wrong. It destroyed the stability of the industry under the justification that the studios monopolized the picture business. But they didn't have a monopoly; there was intense competition that worked well for everybody."[10] This federal antitrust action occurred during the same time that Reagan, as president of the SAG, was defending Hollywood against what he considered overzealous politicians in Washington. Although Reagan was taking action against Communist infiltration in Hollywood, especially of the SAG, he argued that the federal government sometimes went too far in attempting to uncover Communist activity in Hollywood. Noonan notes that "Reagan accused Washington of being drawn by the glamour and lights of the movies."[11] Reagan himself noted that "some members of the House Un-American Activities Committee came to Hollywood searching more for personal publicity than they were for Communists. Many fine people were accused wrongly of being Communists simply because they were liberals."[12] And so Reagan's image of the federal government was gradually being changed into one that was less favorable and less positive. His experience with the progressive tax code in the postwar years would also reinforce this emerging image of the federal government.

Like many military personnel during World War II, Reagan chose to defer his income tax until after the war. Consequently, Reagan recalls that he "returned to civilian life with a good income, a high tax rate, and a debt."[13] He was hoping the debt would be forgiven by the government, but it was not.

Reagan considered these early postwar years to be among his prime earning years in the motion picture industry, yet he felt his work was penalized severely, not just by the tax debt but by the high marginal tax rates of the period. Reagan concluded from this experience that "at the peak of my career at Warner Brothers, I was in the ninety-four percent tax bracket; that meant that after a certain point, I received only six cents of each dollar I earned and the government got the rest. The IRS took such a big chunk of my earnings that after a while I began asking myself whether it was worth it to keep on taking work. Something was wrong with a system like that: When you have to give up such a large percentage of your income in taxes, incentive to work goes down. . . . If I decided to do one less picture, that meant other people at the studio in lower tax brackets wouldn't work as much either; the effect filtered down, and there were fewer total jobs available."[14]

Reagan's experiences with the federal government, stretching over a decade and a half, combined to alter his largely favorable view of the federal government. Notwithstanding the fact that Reagan continued to think of himself as a liberal and a New Deal Democrat, and though he had a number of separate grievances against the federal government, he still did not have a coherent political philosophy at that time. However, a revised and sketchy image of the federal government was beginning to emerge for Reagan during the late 1940s and throughout the early 1950s. The image was of a federal government that had an intrinsic appetite to grow and intrude, often unjustly, into private lives and organizations—areas best left alone by Washington.

Reagan's New Deal Liberalism

Although by 1948 Reagan had experienced several incidents that had eroded some of his confidence in the federal government, he was not yet ready to jettison the New Deal and the legacy of FDR. This was evident in the 1948 presidential election, which presented three candidates to the American people: incumbent Democrat Harry Truman, Republican Thomas Dewey, and Progressive Henry Wallace. Wallace had been vice president under Truman but had left the Democratic Party because of Truman's hard-line position against the Soviet Union and his tepid domestic policy agenda. Consequently, many liberal Democrats who believed Truman held an unduly harsh posture toward our former World War II ally, as well as those who wished for a more aggressive domestic federal policy agenda, defected and supported Wallace's candidacy. Since Reagan's anti-Communist views were well developed by this time and the New Deal was adequate for his domestic policy

views, Wallace offered no appeal to Reagan. If Reagan had been highly liberal and from the left wing of the Democratic Party, he would have supported Wallace. However, Reagan's more moderate leanings suggested a
choice between Truman and Dewey, and Reagan unhesitatingly voted in
1948 for Truman. Why? At this time, though clearly anti-Communist, Reagan still considered himself a New Deal Democrat, and Truman was FDR's
natural successor—the one candidate in the 1948 campaign that offered
the best hope of perpetuating FDR's legacy. Moreover, Reagan was satisfied
with Truman's hard-line foreign policy position toward the Soviet Union.
He felt comfortable campaigning for Truman and ultimately voted for him.
Lou Cannon notes that "[Reagan's] 1948 speeches for President Truman
and other Democrats emphasized such economic issues as Republican in-
flation more than anti-Communism."[15] Reagan's commitment to mainstream Democratic Party beliefs was reflected at this time not only in the
support he offered to Truman and other Democratic Party candidates but
also in the interest that some Democrats had in recruiting Reagan himself
to run for Congress. Lee Edwards notes that "Democrats had attempted to
persuade Ronald Reagan to run for Congress in the late forties—against
Congressman Donald Jackson, a member, of all things, of the House Committee on Un-American Activities. Reagan rejected the Democratic offer."[16] Even so, his support and campaign assistance for other Democratic
candidates continued.

In 1950, Reagan supported a highly devoted New Deal liberal in a famous
U.S. Senate race in California that is still discussed today. The Democratic
candidate who received Reagan's support was former actress Helen Gahagan
Douglas, and her Republican opponent was Richard Nixon. Reagan supported Douglas largely because of her close identification with FDR and the
New Deal. He also knew Douglas and her husband much better than he
knew Nixon. Douglas had established a well-known reputation as a "powerful liberal member of Congress"[17] since being elected to the U.S. House of
Representatives in 1944. She represented a Los Angeles district (fourteenth)
in the House, where she "fought for low-cost housing, price controls, civil
rights, and worked diligently on the Foreign Affairs Committee [House] to
help shape President Harry S. Truman's foreign policy program."[18] On the
other hand, Douglas's anti-Communist credentials were weak, particularly in
contrast to Nixon's, and Nixon capitalized on this vulnerability by dubbing
her the "pink lady" to suggest her close ideological association with the "red"
Communists. Nevertheless, Reagan supported Douglas over Nixon. In Reagan's own words, he says, "As a liberal Democrat, I was naturally opposed to
Richard Nixon. In 1950, he ran for a seat in the U.S. Senate from California

against Congresswoman Helen Gahagan Douglas, the wife of an actor-friend of mine, Melvyn Douglas, and I campaigned against him. Nixon won after a bitter battle that focused on allegations Helen Douglas was a Communist sympathizer. In those days I worked on the campaigns of just about any Democrat who was willing to accept my help."[19] Reagan's observation is an accurate one, but, ironically, 1950 would be the last year he would support the Democratic Party ticket in toto.[20] Of course, in 1952 Reagan would support the Eisenhower candidacy, but not before first trying to recruit him to run as a Democrat. When that effort failed, Reagan recalls that "when Ike decided to run on the Republican ticket, I decided: If I considered him the best man for the job as a Democrat, he still ought to be my choice. So I campaigned and voted for Ike—my first for a Republican."[21] And although Reagan supported and voted for Ike in 1952, Reagan's domestic policy views continued to be characterized as liberal, in fact even too liberal for the Los Angeles County Democratic Central Committee. According to Frank Mankiewicz, a liberal member of the Los Angeles County Democratic Central Committee, the committee "declined to endorse Reagan as a prospective Democratic candidate for an open House seat because he was considered too liberal."[22] And even the following year, in 1953, Reagan is reported to have supported a Democrat for the nonpartisan mayorship of Los Angeles.[23]

Reagan's campaign support and voting record during the late 1940s and early 1950s suggests that the evolution of his domestic policy views, especially regarding federalism and the political economy (i.e., government taxation, regulation), was gradual. It would require the remainder of the decade of the 1950s to complete the evolution, and substantial impetus to that evolution would be provided by Reagan's experiences while employed with General Electric. That employment relationship was crucial to Reagan's political development and his growing understanding that American freedom was threatened not only by Communism but by growth in American government as well. He began working for General Electric in 1954, two years after his marriage to Nancy and at a time when his acting career was in decline. His relationship with GE would run from 1954 to 1962 and would provide, in Reagan's words, "almost a postgraduate course in political science for me."[24]

The General Electric Years

On the eve of Ronald Reagan's election to the presidency in November 1980, *Newsweek* magazine ran a special report entitled "Ronald Reagan Up Close," which noted that "[Reagan's] eight-year tour with GE became his apprenticeship in politics—a movable rehearsal for his rise from novice to nominee for President in a decade and a half."[25] That apprenticeship included valuable experience that allowed Reagan the opportunity to hone a variety of skills important for a successful political career, but it also included a dynamic process in which Reagan's thinking about domestic policy issues came to fruition. Still considering himself a liberal and a New Deal Democrat when he was hired by General Electric in 1954, Reagan would begin to "associate with men of wealth and corporate power . . . with, as Reagan described, a trade-union chip on his shoulder."[26] He was obviously referring here to his prolabor values instilled during his early family life, affirmed by FDR and the New Deal, and reinforced with his experience as president of the Screen Actors Guild. However, Ronald Reagan would soon discover, according to his brother, Neil, that "not all board chairmen [were] robber barons."[27] Nor, as he was already learning, were all public officials angels— particularly those who advocated a more expansive federal role to "help" the people.

Taft Schreiber first approached Ronald Reagan about working for General Electric in 1954. Schreiber proposed that Reagan host a new television program, *General Electric Theater*, and also function as GE's "goodwill ambassador" from the home office to the GE plants around the country. Reagan jumped at the opportunity and accepted the GE offer, which would develop into a lucrative contract for the discouraged actor whose career at the time was at its nadir. Reagan estimates that during his eight years with GE, he visited all 135 plants and met 250,000 employees. Further, "Two of the eight years were spent traveling, and with speeches sometimes running at fourteen a day, [Reagan] was on his feet in front of a microphone for about 250,000 minutes."[28]

During these visits, Reagan was expected to build the morale of GE employees and to assist in linking more effectively the GE plants with their respective communities. These were particularly important tasks for GE, since it had significantly decentralized operations in order to achieve higher levels of productivity, but at the risk of potential morale problems such as the loss of employee identity and connectedness with the company. Reagan himself observed that "sending the host of the GE *Theater* to the far-flung plants . . . would demonstrate that the New York office cared about company employees no matter where they were and would also help forge a closer link between the plants and the communities where they were located. Local managers were instructed to take me to local events."[29] During the first year or so of plant visits, Reagan simply walked the assembly lines at the GE plants and spoke informally to small groups of employees. These groups varied significantly and included secretaries, management officials, shop workers, professional engineers, technical workers, and others.[30] Naturally, Reagan was recognized by employees at the plants as a Hollywood celebrity, and so his main topic during these talks was Hollywood and the motion picture industry. Reagan recalls, "I'd speak to them in small groups from a platform set up on the floor of the factories; I'd tell them a little about Hollywood and our show [*General Electric Theater*], throw it open to questions, then move on to another plant."[31] These talks were informal and spontaneous and covered a variety of Reagan's experiences in Hollywood. Reagan recalls that these initial visits included talks with "a brief greeting and explanation of why I was there, which of necessity had to be fairly pat, but then I freewheeled my way into a question-and-answer session and that really made for variety. One group would get off on the subject of stunts in movies, and how the fights were done; another (particularly the gals) wanted to know about what we did on Saturday night—and so it went."[32]

After some period of visiting only plants and talking to GE employees, Reagan began developing the community relations component of his work. He did this with the assistance of Earl Dunckel, a GE executive who accompanied Reagan on the visits. As Lee Edwards notes, "The community relations part of his job started more slowly but in a few months he was talking to dozens of civic and educational organizations about Hollywood, the *real* Hollywood."[33] To Reagan, the *real* Hollywood was far different from the Hollywood portrayed by the media. *Real* Hollywood was far more ethical than the media had been presenting to the American people. To the new audiences of community and service groups, Reagan delivered an effective defense for the entertainment industry and talked more broadly about his experiences in Hollywood, such as the government's excessively high rates of taxation on his and other Hollywood professionals' income; government overregulation of the industry, such as its antitrust action; and, of course, his earlier experience with Communist infiltration within the industry. Reagan would warn his audiences that his experience was not unique and that "if they weren't careful, people in other occupations might soon find themselves in the same fix as those of us in Hollywood and be denied fair treatment by the government: If it could happen to people in the picture business, [Reagan] said, it could happen to people in any business."[34] In the same vein, Reagan warned that Communist infiltration was not unique to Hollywood and that it could threaten other industries and other sectors of America. Audience reaction to Reagan's warning about Communism surprised him. Reagan was "dumbfounded to discover how completely uninformed the average audience was concerning internal Communism and how it operated. He was determined to educate them, and in the process, his speeches began to concentrate more and more on Communism and collectivism."[35]

During this time, audiences learned from Reagan—but Reagan was also learning from his audiences. Through his interaction with GE executives, employees, and community activists, Reagan discovered thousands of Americans who were not only concerned about Communism but who, after hearing of Reagan's experience with the federal government in Hollywood, were also concerned about a growing federal government that was overly intrusive and that threatened individual liberty in America. Many of these people would approach Reagan after a speech and tell him about their own negative experiences with the federal government. Reagan recalls, "After I began including these remarks [his experience with the federal government in Hollywood] in the speeches, an interesting thing happened: No matter where I was, I'd find people from the audience waiting to talk to me after a speech and they'd all say, 'hey, if you think things are bad in your business, let me tell you what is happening in my business . . .' I'd listen and they'd cite examples of government interference and snafus and complain how bureaucrats, through over regulation, were telling them how to run their businesses. . . . I heard complaints about how the ever-expanding federal government was encroaching on liberties we'd always taken for granted."[36] Reagan learned from these countless interactions with people in his audiences that "they are concerned, not with security as some would have us believe, but with their very firm personal liberties."[37]

It was during this time, approximately the second year of his contract with General Electric, that although Reagan was relaying anecdotes and stories about his experiences in Hollywood, he was still without a coherent philosophy of government. There appeared to be no unifying themes to his messages. Dinesh D'Souza recognized this when he observed that "[Reagan's] philosophy was an inchoate assortment of horror stories and personal incidents that Reagan picked up in his travels. People regularly told him about how their attempts to improve their lives were frustrated by high taxation and arbitrary and burdensome regulations. Reagan believed these stories because he heard them again and again, and he saw that they were not the product of theorizing but were based on experience. Recognizing their narrative power, he began to integrate them into his own presentations, often buttressed by news items and quips that illustrated his themes."[38] In fact, as Bill Boyarsky has noted, when Reagan was forty-five (in 1956), two years into his employment contract with GE, he still apparently had not arrived at a clearly defined political philosophy. Boyarsky notes that GE president Ralph Cordiner became concerned over Reagan's difficulties in answering audiences' questions and told him, "You'd better get yourself a philosophy, something you can stand for and something you think this country stands for."[39] Cordiner believes that "this is when he really started to change."[40]

His audiences continued to change as well. As Reagan himself recalls, "By the third year the tours were being scheduled around the speaking engagements and the routine weekly luncheon clubs had given way to the more important annual events: state Chamber of Commerce banquets, national conventions, and groups recognized as important political sounding boards such as the Executives Club of Chicago."[41] As his audience changed and broadened, so did his message. Reagan recalls that "the Hollywood portion of the talk shortened and disappeared. The warning words of what could happen changed to concrete examples of what has already happened, and I learned very early to document those examples."[42] As the Hollywood portion of the talk shortened and disappeared, so did the Hollywood anecdotes and experiences. What emerged instead was a powerful and coherent philosophy and message with well-documented evidence to support it. That message drew together Reagan's own experience with the federal government, the experiences of others with the federal government relayed to Reagan on the GE speaking tour, and Reagan's own research on the matter. The array of evidence would now be tied together by Reagan to support a coherent argument that the U.S. federal bureaucracy was growing ever larger, that it was wasteful and inefficient, and that it was increasingly threatening American freedom. Moreover, it was intrinsically incapable of policing itself and limiting its own growth—restraint upon growth would have to be imposed from without rather than from within. Reagan recalls that this became an important theme in his message when he states, "I became convinced that some of our fundamental freedoms were in jeopardy because of the emergence of a *permanent government* never envisioned by the framers of the Constitution: a federal bureaucracy that was becoming so powerful it was able to set policy and thwart the desires not only of ordinary citizens, but their elected representatives in Congress."[43] Reagan added that he would "make a note of what people told me [audience experiences], do some research when I got home, and then include some of the examples in my next speech. . . . Pretty soon, [the speech] became basically a warning to people about the threat of government. . . . No government has ever voluntarily reduced itself in size—and that, in a way, became my theme."[44]

And so Reagan's emerging message was not a mindless antigovernment diatribe as some have characterized it. Rather, it was the product of several years of Reagan's own experience combined with similar experiences conveyed to him by others during the GE speeches and with research Reagan undertook on his own. Without sophisticated and rigorous analysis but relying upon personal experience and shared stories with others, Reagan identified the federal bureaucracy as the primary problem. It would be left to others to conduct the rigorous analysis to support what Reagan had discovered through experience and common sense.

Public Choice

The task of providing the scholarly analysis to buttress Reagan's argument about the federal bureaucracy would fall to a genre of economists that emerged after World War II who would apply economic assumptions and methods to various political activities. Their approach would become known as "public choice" and would include some of the finest minds in the discipline of economics.

One leading public choice scholar has succinctly defined his methodological approach as "the economic study of nonmarket decision making, or simply the application of economics to political science. The subject matter of public choice is the same as that of political science: the theory of the state, voting rules, voter behavior, party politics, the bureaucracy, and so on. The methodology of public choice is that of economics, however. The basic behavioral postulate of public choice, as for economics, is that man is an egoistic, rational, utility maximizer."[45] Perhaps the best-known public choice economist is Professor James Buchanan of George Mason University, who has been called the "founding father of public choice."[46] Buchanan won the Nobel Prize in economic sciences in 1986 for his public choice research, particularly his work in applying economic principles of exchange to political decision making. Buchanan has enhanced the world's understanding of political processes through his innovation, creativity, and rigor, all of which are apparent in his classic 1962 book *Calculus of Consent*, coauthored with Gordon Tullock.

Since public choice economists study a variety of political activities, it wasn't long before some of these researchers began to examine governmental bureaucracy. Clearly, one of the first public choice economists to study governmental bureaucracy was Gordon Tullock. In a fashion similar to Reagan's, Tullock had experienced the dysfunctions of governmental bureaucracy. For Tullock, however, his experience had been within the foreign service hierarchy over a nine-year period. After his postgraduate training in economics, Tullock's earlier experience with governmental bureaucracy became the basis for his 1965 book *The Politics of Bureaucracy*. The work contributed valuable insights about governmental bureaucracies. As Buchanan noted in his tribute to Tullock, "The substantive contribution in the manuscript was centered on the hypothesis that, regardless of role, the individual bureaucrat responds to the rewards and punishments that he confronts. . . . The economic

theory of bureaucracy was born, one that has since been considerably en-
riched by Downs (1967), Niskanen (1975), Breton and Wintrobe (1982),
and others."[47] And so the emerging economic theory of bureaucracy would
posit that the bureaucrat, like others, had a human nature that was egoistic,
rational, and utility maximizing, or, in other words, basically self-interested.
Examining the organizational incentives confronting bureaucrats would
therefore help explain the behavior of governmental bureaucracies.

In his book *Bureaucracy and Representative Government* published in 1971,
William Niskanen made a major contribution to our understanding of governmental bureaucracy. His work has been described as the "first systematic
effort to study bureaucracies within a public choice framework."[48] In this
classic book, Niskanen argues that bureaucrats maximize their utility by seeking more prestige, power, and pay. Of course the primary means of accom-
plishing this goal is by budget expansion, which leads to inflated costs, higher
levels of inefficiency, and excessive growth in government.[49] Moreover,
Niskanen's assessment of rewards and penalties within governmental bureaucracies leads him to conclude that budgetary expansion (i.e., governmental
bureaucratic growth) is rewarded, and controlling costs is penalized. Thus
governmental bureaucracies will have serious limitations in controlling un-
necessary and unneeded growth. Niskanen's assessment has been affirmed by
a host of public choice economists conducting their own theoretical and em-
pirical analysis of governmental bureaucracies. Gordon Tullock, James Ben-
nett, Manuel Johnson, Thomas Borcherding, James Buchanan, and others
have all built upon the work of Niskanen.

Public choice economists have clearly made a substantial impact on the
scholarly study of governmental bureaucracies since World War II. This economic school of thought is not without its critics, however, both within and
outside the discipline of economics. Political scientists and economists such
as John Donahue, Steven Kelman, Ruth DeHoog, and others have argued
against public choice assumptions and findings. The debate will continue
among scholars from a variety of academic fields.

Notwithstanding this scholarly debate, public choice economists have
provided an enormous amount of credibility to the argument Reagan developed during his General Electric years—that is, that the federal government
has a rapacious appetite, that the federal bureaucracy's growth is substantially
self-serving, and that the bureaucracy lacks the capacity to control and limit
its own growth. A variety of distinguished public choice economists have advanced this argument as well, including a Nobel Prize winner. But remember,
Reagan was making this argument during the 1950s and early to mid-1960s.
This was not a time when Reagan's message would have been particularly

popular in many parts of the country, especially during the Great Society era of the Johnson administration during the mid-1960s. However, Reagan's message was clearly a warning about federal bureaucracy and its growth, and it preceded most of the rigorous scholarly studies by public choice economists who came to most of the same conclusions Reagan did. What Reagan lacked in methodological rigor he made up for with experience, intuition, and common sense. He discovered during his years with General Electric a growing and encroaching federal government understood primarily as a powerful, unelected bureaucracy that was increasingly removed from and unresponsive to the people it was meant to serve. And, to a greater degree than most public choice economists, Reagan would evaluate this trend in moral terms and would conclude that individual liberty was threatened by this imbalance in the American federal system. To Reagan, the American people had to be alerted to a growing federal bureaucracy that was not just producing economic waste and inefficiency but was also presenting a growing threat to individual freedom. Reagan comprehended that the core issue he had discovered during his time with General Electric struck at the very root of America's identity. It was his duty as an American patriot to sound the alarm about this second threat to American freedom just as he had warned of the earlier Communist threat.

What Reagan Learned about the Encroaching Federal Government

The concepts of balance in political science (checks and balances), equilibrium in economics (supply and demand), and homeostasis in biology (organism viability) are extremely important. In each of these disciplines, as in most of life, a proper balance among competing forces is important for maintaining a system's viability and effectiveness. This is true whatever the nature of the system. However, when imbalance or disequilibrium occurs within a complex system, deleterious effects are likely to ensue. This is what Ronald Reagan believed he had discovered about the American federal system during the 1950s. Although his learning was gradual, Reagan eventually became convinced that an overly intrusive federal bureaucracy was damaging to the federal balance between national and state governments and threatened to erode individual freedoms. Reagan's argument seemed to be an echo from the past—that is, Reagan's argument resembled the earlier Anti-Federalist argument from the inception of the republic about a powerful central government threatening states' rights and individual liberty. But the argument also reactivated Jeffersonian principles of states' rights and limited government that had long been dormant in American public discourse. Reagan thought the argument highly relevant to the circumstances the American people were encountering during the 1950s and beyond.

The 1950s were a period of transformation for Ronald Reagan. His experiences during this decade, particularly those linked to his employment with General Electric, provided a major source of learning about a second threat to American freedom: a growing and overly intrusive federal government. And although this learning process would come later and take longer than his discovery about the Communist threat, Reagan would still regard the threat of the federal government as one that needed to be publicly identified and confronted. From his many experiences with General Electric during the 1950s, Reagan learned much about this threat to American freedom, but four important lessons can be clearly identified since they became the basis for most of his speeches during this period.

First, and perhaps most fundamental, Reagan learned that a growing federal bureaucracy—with its ostensible purpose of "caring" for the American people—posed a real threat to individual freedom. Reagan learned not just from GE executives but from GE employees and community activists that the federal government was overly intrusive in their lives and restricted their freedom through excessive regulations and taxes. These reports resonated with Reagan's own earlier experience with the federal government. Interestingly, Reagan made no distinction between economic and political freedom. He saw the interdependence between the two and believed that threats to economic freedom (e.g., high taxation) presented threats to political freedom and that threats to political freedom presented threats to economic freedom. Reagan once argued, "It is time we realized that profit, property and freedom are inseparable. You cannot have one of them without the others."[50] To Reagan, the concept of freedom was indivisible: Freedom could not be threatened anywhere without threatening freedom everywhere. Moreover, in his assessment that American freedom was threatened by an encroaching federal government, Reagan consistently identified the federal bureaucracy as the primary source of the threat. Like the public choice economists that followed him, Reagan was skeptical of "altruistic" motives categorically imputed to bureaucrats. Bureaucrats often pursued their own agendas at the public's expense. This meant excessive spending and uncontrolled growth that the bureaucracy was helpless to restrain. For Reagan, restraint would have to be imposed from without by elected officials who truly served the people.

Second, Reagan learned that liberalism once again seemed incapable of recognizing a genuine threat to American freedom. Just as liberalism had failed to recognize the Communist threat to freedom, it also failed to recognize that a growing and so-called benevolent federal bureaucracy represented a threat to freedom as well. Reagan criticized the liberalism that endorsed and perpetuated big government in *both* political parties. In his second autobiography, for instance, he stated, "I'm not so sure I changed as much as the *parties* changed."[51] However, Reagan would eventually identify New Deal liberalism within the Democratic Party as the locus of the problem. As Nancy Reagan recalled in her memoir, "As he traveled across the country for General Electric, Ronnie started seeing things differently. He became increasingly concerned about government interference in the free enterprise system—and also in the lives of individuals. One day he came home from a speaking trip and told me he was starting to realize that the Democrats he had campaigned for in election years were responsible for the very things he was speaking out against between elections."[52] Reagan did not ascribe treasonous motives to liberals but instead castigated them for foolishly and naively believing that government activism and growth would somehow bring about a better society. Instead, Reagan saw both threats, at home and abroad, as gathering and related forces of tyranny.

Third, because Reagan saw threats to freedom where liberals failed to see them, Reagan revised his views about liberalism. His revised understanding of liberalism led him to conclude that liberals viewed Communism as simply an extreme form of liberalism: To liberals, the difference between liberalism and Communism was a difference in degree, not in kind. To Reagan, this view permitted many liberals during the Cold War years to think that a convergence of our system and the Soviet system was possible—perhaps even desirable—in order to avoid nuclear war. The American political and economic systems simply had to move to the left by promoting an expanded role for the federal government at home, and the Soviet system could accommodate by moving to the right. Then nuclear war between the two superpowers could be avoided, since the two systems would come to more closely resemble one another. Reagan believed many liberals held this fatally flawed view. He believed no accommodation was possible and that inevitably freedom or tyranny would prevail.

Finally, Reagan learned during his time with General Electric that thousands upon thousands of Americans shared his views. These were not simply General Electric employees but thousands of community activists throughout the country as well. He believed that his views were not radical but rather resonated with mainstream America. Although his public-speaking ability improved during this period, Reagan believed that it was not his speaking technique but rather the substance of his message about freedom that resonated with his audiences. His speeches were altered from time to time with new evidence and anecdotes, but the message remained the same: Freedom was being threatened by Communism and an encroaching federal bureaucracy, the people must be alerted to these threats, and action must be taken to reduce or eliminate them. The American people must see, according to Reagan, that these two threats to American freedom had a common link: they were gradually growing, and they both represented the same manifestation of tyranny—elite rule over the people, whether that rule came from abroad (Communism) or from within (the federal government).

Reagan's experiences with both threats would be fundamental in transforming his political views. However, Reagan felt other influences during this period that served to reinforce what he had learned about Communism and the federal bureaucracy. Although these reinforcing influences were secondary to Reagan's political transformation, they deserve close examination. These secondary influences of family, friends, and intellectuals helped convince Reagan that he was on the right track in exposing threats to and proposing protections for American freedom.

Notes

1. Lou Cannon, *Reagan* (New York: G. P. Putnam's Sons, 1982), 94.
2. Ronald Reagan, *An American Life* (New York: Simon & Schuster, 1990), 130.
3. Peggy Noonan, *When Character Was King* (New York: Viking Press, 2001), 84.
4. Ronald Reagan and Richard Hubler, *Where's the Rest of Me?* (New York: Dell, 1965), 64.
5. Lee Edwards, *Reagan: A Political Biography* (San Diego: Viewpoint, 1967), 30.
6. Ibid., 49.
7. Ronald Reagan and Richard Hubler, *Where's the Rest of Me?* 144.
8. Ibid., 145, emphasis added.
9. Ibid., 146.
10. Ronald Reagan, *An American Life*, 117.
11. Peggy Noonan, *When Character Was King*, 64.
12. Ronald Reagan, *An American Life*, 114.
13. Ronald Reagan and Richard Hubler, *Where's the Rest of Me?* 279.
14. Ronald Reagan, *An American Life*, 231.
15. Lou Cannon, *President Reagan: The Role of a Lifetime* (New York: Simon & Schuster, 1991), 286.

16. Lee Edwards, *Reagan: A Political Biography*, 76–77.

17. Ingrid Scobie, "Douglas v Nixon: A Campaign on the Conscience," *History Today*, November 1992, 16–17.

18. Ibid.

19. Ronald Reagan, *An American Life*, 132.

20. Lee Edwards, *Reagan: A Political Biography*, 74n.

21. Ronald Reagan, *An American Life*, 133.

22. Lou Cannon, *President Reagan: The Role of a Lifetime*, 286.

23. James David Barber, *The Presidential Character: Predicting Performance in the White House* (Englewood Cliffs, NJ: Prentice Hall, 1985), 476.

24. Ronald Reagan, *An American Life*, 129.

25. Gerald Lubenow, Martin Kasindorf, Frank Maier, James Doyle, and other *Newsweek* correspondents, "Ronald Reagan Up Close," *Newsweek*, July 21, 1980, 36.

26. Ibid.

27. Ibid.

28. Ronald Reagan and Richard Hubler, *Where's the Rest of Me?* 293.

29. Ronald Reagan, *An American Life*, 127.

30. Lee Edwards, *Reagan: A Political Biography*, 69–70.

31. Ronald Reagan, *An American Life*, 127.

32. Ronald Reagan and Richard Hubler, *Where's the Rest of Me?* 294.

33. Lee Edwards, *Reagan: A Political Biography*, 66–67.

34. Ronald Reagan, *An American Life*, 128–29.

35. Lee Edwards, *Reagan: A Political Biography*, 67.

36. Ronald Reagan, *An American Life*, 129.

37. Ronald Reagan and Richard Hubler, *Where's the Rest of Me?* 295.

38. Dinesh D'Souza, *Ronald Reagan: How an Ordinary Man Became an Extraordinary Leader* (New York: Free Press, 1997), 48.

39. Bill Boyarsky, *The Rise of Ronald Reagan* (New York: Random House, 1968), 26.

40. Ibid.

41. Ronald Reagan and Richard Hubler, *Where's the Rest of Me?* 303–4.

42. Ibid., 303.

43. Ronald Reagan, *An American Life*, 129, emphasis in original.

44. Ibid.

45. Dennis C. Mueller, *Public Choice* (Cambridge: Cambridge University Press, 1979), 1.

46. Iain McLean, *Public Choice: An Introduction* (New York: Basil Blackwell, 1987), vii.

47. James M. Buchanan, "The Qualities of a Natural Economist," in *Democracy and Public Choice: Essays in Honor of Gordon Tullock*, ed. Charles K. Rowley (New York: Basil Blackwell, 1987), 11.

48. Dennis C. Mueller, *Public Choice*, 156.

49. William Niskanen, *Bureaucracy and Representative Government* (Chicago: Aldine-Atherton, 1971).

50. Lou Cannon, *President Reagan: The Role of a Lifetime*, 90.

51. Ronald Reagan, *An American Life*, 134.

52. Nancy Reagan, *My Turn: The Memoirs of Nancy Reagan* (New York: Random House, 1989), 129.

~

CHAPTER FOUR

Family and Friends

During Ronald Reagan's journey from Democrat to Republican, he acquired innumerable acquaintances and friends, some of whom had an influence on his political transformation during the 1940s and 1950s. It is difficult if not impossible to conduct an exhaustive study that would identify all influences from family and friends, and even if it were possible, assigning weight to the varying influences would be very difficult. Nevertheless, it is possible to identify a few select family members and friends who most Reagan biographers and scholars would agree were among the most influential in Reagan's political transformation. These individuals interacted in some fashion with Reagan, often through discussions and debates, and thereby contributed to his political development. Although these influences on Reagan were real and palpable, they are obviously difficult to isolate and weigh, since other related and circumstantial influences were occurring simultaneously. Life happens through history, not within a laboratory.

The evidence strongly suggests, however, that a few family members and friends did exercise a secondary or reinforcing influence on Reagan as he journeyed from Democrat to Republican. These were not primary influences, though, since discussions and debates with Reagan produced no immediate effect. There is no evidence that anyone converted Reagan to the Republican Party through argument. Actually, the evidence is to the contrary—that is, Reagan was not converted by arguments but rather he learned primarily from his own direct experiences such as those reviewed in earlier chapters.

However, this is not to say that interaction with family and friends was without influence. Rather, family and friends exercised influence that was more subtle and less palpable than his experience with Communist threats in Hollywood and his later experiences with General Electric. Also, one aspect of the influence of family and friends on Reagan's political development was that it was delayed rather than immediate. Reagan's arguments with family and friends became memories for him, and the arguments he heard opposing Communism and warning of an encroaching federal government made sense later when specific circumstances, such as the Communist threat in Hollywood, became more palpable in his experience.

Two of Reagan's personality traits impeded the influence of family and friends to some degree. For one thing, Reagan's well-known "stubbornness streak," which often proved to be an asset during his presidency (particularly in not conceding SDI at Reykjavik and in not conceding to Democrats his proposed tax cuts in the 1981 budget), may have hindered his learning from the arguments of family and friends. Reagan's journey from Democrat to Republican was gradual—spanning about fifteen years—in spite of the many Republican arguments he heard and with which he would later agree. Reagan's stubbornness accounts to some degree for the delay in his journey. A second trait that impeded the influence of family and friends was Reagan's propensity to avoid close relationships. Reagan has been described by many, including his wife Nancy, as a remote person—a person difficult to know. In her memoir, My Turn, Nancy Reagan observed, "Although he loves people, he often seems remote, and he doesn't let anybody get too close. There's a wall around him. He lets me come closer than anyone else, but there are times when even I feel that barrier."[1] Although Reagan had many friends, very few were close friends. This trait contributed as well to the diminished influence by family and friends.

Overview

Like most people, Ronald Reagan's journey through life included dynamic changes in his family relationships and friendships. He maintained his relationships with his biological family even after moving to Hollywood, but eventually his marriage to Nancy Davis would graft him into the Davis family and a new set of relationships. Reagan kept many of his early friendships, but not all, and of course he made new friends along the way. However, those family members and friends who especially influenced Reagan's journey from Democrat to Republican did so through their interaction with him sometime between 1940 and 1962. Within this context, early relationships with key family members and friends during the 1940s were particularly important in shaping Reagan's view of the Communist threat. Most scholars and biographers of Reagan would agree that four relationships were particularly influential during the early years of his political development: his older brother, Neil, and his friends Dick Powell, Justin Dart, and George Murphy. With the exception of his brother, Ronald Reagan met these men either just before or after 1940, and Reagan respected each one. Moreover, all four men were conservative Republicans who enjoyed arguing politics with Reagan, just as he enjoyed arguing with them. Their discussions and debates with Reagan during the 1940s influenced his hard-line views toward Communism by the decade's end and planted the seeds of thought about the dangers of an encroaching federal government, which would later germinate during the 1950s.

A new set of family members and friends emerged during the 1950s to reinforce Reagan's views about Communism and chip away at his retention of New Deal liberalism. Reagan's marriage to Nancy Davis in 1952 introduced him to his conservative Republican father-in-law, Loyal Davis. Through Davis, Reagan met and got to know Barry Goldwater. Reagan respected both Davis and Goldwater. They were accomplished men. But, like his earlier friendships, both men were conservative Republicans who discussed and debated politics with Reagan on numerous occasions. Given this later time frame (the 1950s), Davis, Goldwater, and Reagan agreed among themselves about the Communist threat to America. Reagan's political differences with Davis and Goldwater were largely over domestic policy, or, to be more precise, Reagan's loyalty to FDR and the New Deal. However, only two years after his marriage to Nancy, Reagan signed with General Electric and began his eight-year employment relationship with the corporate giant. Out of this experience with General Electric, as we discovered in chapter 3, Reagan began to strongly oppose an encroaching federal government. The final chapter in his journey from Democrat to Republican was complete by 1962.

An important friend, however, would accelerate the completion of this final chapter of Reagan's political odyssey. That friend was Earl Dunckel, a General Electric executive who not only accompanied Reagan to General Electric plants and community functions but also argued and advanced his conservative beliefs during the late stages of Reagan's liberalism. Altogether, these eight family members and friends played an influential role in Reagan's journey from Democrat to Republican. Although all were Republican, some played larger roles than others. Altogether, they did not convert Reagan simply by their arguments. Their personal qualities—their character, credibility, and friendship—assisted in reinforcing truths Reagan discovered for himself through his Hollywood and GE experiences.

Early Family and Friends—1940s

In his first autobiography, Ronald Reagan said that at the time he was leaving the military in 1945, he "was not sharp about Communism."[2] At this particular time, Reagan considered himself to be a liberal Democrat with special loyalty to FDR and the New Deal. Reagan held to these views in spite of having heard Republican arguments to the contrary by his older brother, Neil, and his relatively new but good friends Dick Powell, Justin Dart, and George Murphy. All were Republicans. In fact, Neil Reagan had left the Democratic Party in 1933 and had registered that same year as a Republican. Neil Reagan had opposed the New Deal in the early 1930s, and during the 1940s, he would increasingly warn of the Communist threat to America.

Dick Powell has been described as Ronald Reagan's first friend among the movie stars.[3] Only one year after he arrived in Hollywood, Reagan met Powell for the first time on the set of *Hollywood Hotel* in 1938. This was Reagan's second film, and he had a minor role as a newscaster. Dick Powell had the lead role, and he demonstrated genuine interest in and kindness toward young Reagan. As Reagan recalled, "I found myself playing a radio announcer in *Hollywood Hotel*. The star was one of the top box-office figures in Hollywood, Dick Powell, who couldn't have been nicer. Without realizing just how it happened, I found myself in one of the canvas director's chairs usually reserved for the stars and principals. Dick somehow, easily and smoothly, had drawn me into the inner circle as if I had more than two and a half lines. I was one of thousands who were drawn to this very kind man, and who would think of him as a best friend. Sometimes our paths took us in different directions and months would pass without our seeing each other. Still in these later years, when we did meet again, it would be as if no interruption had occurred. I cannot recall Dick ever saying an unkind word about anyone. He always seemed to feel such genuine pleasure at seeing you, and he had a habit of greeting you with the line 'God love you.' It was quite a while before it really penetrated my consciousness that when Dick said it, it wasn't just an expression—he meant it."[4]

However, Reagan's respect for Powell increased immeasurably when in the same year young Reagan would be invited to join the Screen Actors Guild and would "accept with awe and pleasure." Reagan had immense respect for the board members of the SAG, as he recalled in his early autobiography, "The ones who made SAG work in the early days were the ones that didn't need it: Eddie Cantor, Edward Arnold, Ralph Morgan, Robert Montgomery, James Cagney, Walter Pidgeon, George Murphy, Harpo Marx, Cary Grant, Charles Boyer, Dick Powell—and a hundred other stars who could call their own tunes on screen salaries. They were willing to use their personal power in order to better the lot of their fellow actors."[5] Reagan viewed these board members as competent, successful, self-sacrificing, and noble. He would be honored to join their number. And of course two of these early members would become close friends of Reagan's: George Murphy and Dick Powell. Moreover, when Reagan rejoined the SAG board after his military duty in 1946, George Murphy and Dick Powell would be there to welcome him back.

As they got to know each other, Reagan and Powell discovered a mutual interest in politics. They argued often, and amazingly their friendship grew stronger. Powell's widow, June Allyson, recalled that "they had made many films together [by 1941], but arguing politics drew them together. It was a riot to listen to Ronnie, a staunch Democrat, trying to convert Richard [Powell] while Richard argued just as hard to turn Ronnie Republican."[6] Powell advanced arguments not unlike the kind Reagan had had been hearing from his brother, Neil. Powell would often argue that "Roosevelt was *not* the Democratic party; the president's liberal left-wing friends *were*, and the liberal Left was being infiltrated with Communists and fellow travelers. Reagan was naïve if he thought the Democrats were the party of the people. He was being duped, deceived. The Republicans were the true people's party because they had become the keepers of 'the American Way of Life.'"[7] Powell's attempt to separate FDR from the Democratic Party indicates that he learned (probably quickly) that FDR was a hero to young Reagan and that it would be virtually impossible to speak at all disparagingly about the president. Instead, Powell adroitly argued that the president's liberal left-wing friends were taking the party away from its historic roots of representing the people. This argument obviously did not have an immediate effect upon Reagan, but it is reasonably close to Reagan's later argument that he did not leave the Democratic Party; it left him.

When Powell and Reagan argued with one another, however, the general thrust of their debate was to convert one or the other rather than simply to reason and educate. Anne Edwards notes that "whenever Reagan got together with his men friends, the talk would shift to politics. . . . But Reagan's living-room polemics had more to do with an attempt to convert than to reason."[8] Apparently this behavior had an unsettling effect on Reagan's first wife, Jane Wyman, and contributed to some degree to their marital problems. In any case, the two friends exchanged partisan views with the intent of winning and converting. In Powell's case, too, he saw that Reagan had some potential to run as a Republican candidate for office. Powell advanced this view to Reagan in the early 1940s, obviously without success. Nevertheless, out of Reagan's early partisan debates with Powell, Reagan may have believed that

Powell's arguments were attempts to convert him to the Republican Party. Reagan would insist that he would not convert to the Republican Party time and time again when Powell's arguments ran contrary to his own liberal beliefs.

Justin Dart, also a Republican, met Reagan through Dart's second wife, Jane Bryan, in 1940. Bryan and Reagan had been cast together in several films and had gotten to know one another before Bryan introduced Reagan to her husband. Dart and Reagan would develop a growing friendship over the years that would resemble Reagan's other friendships with Dick Powell and George Murphy: clashing politics but mutual respect and confidence in one another. On the eve of Ronald Reagan's election to the presidency, Dart was interviewed by the *New York Times*, and he recalled that when he had first met Reagan, "he [Reagan] was a rabid Democrat. The night we first met we fought like cats and dogs. My wife warned me not to talk politics with him."⁹ Although their politics clashed, Reagan and Dart became fast friends. By 1941, and with Reagan only thirty years old, Dart and Powell were considered close friends of his. By this time, Reagan had been in Hollywood for four years and had been married to Jane Wyman for one year. Reagan did not fit in with many of the Hollywood personalities at the time, but as Anne Edwards notes, "His best friends were his golf buddies and conservative men like actor Dick Powell and businessman Justin Dart, with whom he enjoyed arguing politics."¹⁰ Reagan no doubt heard many of the same arguments from Dart that he had heard from Powell. However, Edwards notes as well that "Justin Dart had a fantastic grasp of economics, and he and Reagan could go around and around debating issues for hours."¹¹ Apparently Dart advanced the public choice argument that a bureaucracy has a tendency to grow and that the New Deal meant a surge of growth in the federal government for the benefit of federal bureaucrats rather than the American people.¹² According to Edwards, Dart's argument had some influence on Reagan, though Reagan maintained his New Deal liberalism for approximately fifteen more years.¹³

However, Justin Dart's influence on Reagan came not only from substantive arguments but from the respect that Reagan had for the man. At the time Dart met Reagan, Dart retained a large business interest in Walgreens Drugs, and over time he would hold high-level executive positions with Rexall Drugs, United Airlines, and Dart & Kraft Inc. For Reagan, Dart's business success over the years would strengthen the credibility of his earlier Republican arguments. However, Reagan did reject outright one Republican argument advanced by both Dart and Powell in 1941: "Dick Powell and Justin Dart had suggested he should consider a congressional race—as a Republican."¹⁴ Five years later, in 1946, the Democrats would approach Reagan with the same offer. Influential people on both sides of the aisle were beginning to recognize Reagan's potential for success in politics. In fact, Powell thought he had much greater potential success in politics than in the motion picture business. On the other hand, after both Powell and Dart advanced political arguments for the purpose of converting Reagan to the Republican Party, Reagan developed the view that partisan arguments contrary to his liberal beliefs were simply attempts to convert him to the Republican Party. Criticism of the New Deal was seen as an attempt at political conversion. Reagan would often advance this argument to his brother, Neil, and to another Republican friend, George Murphy, when they, too, argued and debated with him. Neil Reagan and George Murphy were among those early and lifelong relationships that had an important influence on Ronald Reagan, and because they were not only close to Reagan but also shared with him the experience of defecting from the Democratic to the Republican Party, they warrant special consideration.

A Sibling Relationship

Neil Reagan, born September 16, 1908, in Tampico, Illinois, was Ronald Reagan's older brother by approximately two and a half years. He was Ronald Reagan's only sibling. Neil was known as "Moon" to many family members and friends. His nickname was derived from the Moon Mullins comic strip while he was on the high school football team.[15] Although he would live in the shadow of Ronald Reagan during most of his adult life, Neil lived a productive and successful life. He followed his brother Ronald to Eureka College and graduated with a degree in economics in 1933. Two years later, he married Bess Hoffman and remained married to her for sixty-one years. The couple had no children. Upon Neil Reagan's death on December 11, 1996, the Office of Ronald Reagan issued a press release summarizing many of Neil Reagan's vocational and civic achievements. The press release stated,

> When Ronald Reagan became an announcer at WHO Radio in Des Moines, Iowa, Neil followed him to the sister station, WOC, in Davenport, Iowa, where he served as program director. After Ronald Reagan came to Hollywood and brought his parents to California, he encouraged Neil and Bess to come too. His first job in California was as an announcer at KFWB radio. He then went to work for CBS and from there to McCann-Erickson Advertising Agency, where he became Senior Vice President and head of the Los Angeles office until his retirement in 1973. While with McCann-Erickson, he directed Jean Hersholt in the Doctor Christian show for nearly twenty years. He also directed his brother, Ronald, in Death Valley Days. In 1967, along with Elton

Rule, he was honored by the Western States Advertising Agencies Association as "Leader of the Year" in advertising. Neil Reagan was active in many civic organizations. He served as President of the Hollywood Advertising Club, President of the Los Angeles Advertising Club, [and] President of the Association of the West.[16]

Neil Reagan's considerable achievements reflected his own drive and initiative. The responsible positions he held and the honors he received were due more to his own efforts and abilities than to any preferred status based on his relationship to Ronald Reagan. Actually, the relationship between the two brothers was characterized more by competition and rivalry than by any subservient patronage by Neil to Ronald or vice versa. Neil was clearly his own man. However, the sibling rivalry did not overwhelm the two brothers. Many biographers have described the sibling relationship as a competitive but close one—the brothers helped one another throughout their lives.

Perhaps the competitive nature of the relationship emerged at the very beginning—when Ronald Reagan was born. In an early biography of Ronald Reagan, Neil recalled that he was told, "Now you can go home and see your baby brother. . . . For two days after I was home I would not go in the room where my brother and my mother were. I didn't want any part of a brother. I had been promised a sister by my mother and father. That's all I wanted."[17] As the boys grew, very different personalities and interests emerged. Neil strongly identified with his father, Jack, while Ronald identified more with his mother, Nelle. At a relatively young age, Neil revealed a more boisterous and gregarious personality that resembled Jack's. Neil would also identify with his father's Catholic faith rather than with his mother's Protestant beliefs. By contrast, Ronald was quieter than his older brother and would spend much more time reading or engaged in some solitary activity. Ronald also identified with Nelle's Protestant beliefs. The two boys were quite different, and this difference in personality and temperament was reflected in very different friendships for the two boys.

In an interview, Neil Reagan summed this up quite well when he observed that "his brother made friends wherever he went, but did not seek them out. . . . He had a wide circle of friends at the tail end of grade school and in high school, but he also was quiet and a lot of his activities were partly by himself. . . . I always sort of ran with gangs. He didn't."[18] Neil Reagan's comment is supported by interviews conducted by Garry Wills. In his biography on Reagan, *Reagan's America*, Wills discovered that "in interviewing people who knew the brothers in their youth, or knew their reputations, in Tampico, Dixon, and Eureka, I found them dividing into 'Neil people' and 'Ronald people.' Neil people found him more easygoing than his brother, more fun, more confiding. . . . Ronald was shyer than the expansive 'Irishman' Neil."[19]

Sibling rivalry between the two emerged during their youth and persisted well into their adult years. Perhaps it never went away. Athletics and academics are often sources of sibling rivalry, and the Reagan brothers were no exception to this general rule. As Wills again notes, "Neil regularly tells reporters (with some germ of truth, at least for high school) that he, not Ronald, was the football star."[20] Further, Wills notes that "Neil has even told friends, as he told Tom Bates, 'I was a good student—he wasn't.'"[21]

Commenting on the competitive nature of the Reagan brothers' relationship, Wills notes that "it was a tug-of-war that would not end, not the least because the ties of affection could bear any strain. The brothers would remain close, if competing, and Ronald could afford to be generous where Neil could hardly avoid being jealous."[22] Though a natural rivalry had developed, the brothers still looked after one another. Neil once remembered that "when someone started taking picks at me, he'd [Dutch] stick in, and if somebody started taking picks on him, I'd stick in."[23]

And so a reasonably close yet competitive relationship emerged during the brothers' youth and persisted well into their adult years. Skinner, Anderson, and Anderson have captured this phenomena in their book *Reagan: A Life in Letters* when they write, "Born in 1908, Moon [Neil] was a bit over two years older, and for many years was taller, better at sports, and better in school. But Reagan [Ronald] caught up with Moon and soon eclipsed him, both in height and accomplishment. . . . The two brothers remained close over the years, Moon rising to be a top executive of the McCann-Erickson advertising firm, but they were competitive and Moon seemed to have a glint of envy as Reagan's career soared. They stayed in touch all their lives, and Moon handled the advertising in Reagan's gubernatorial campaign in California, although he was not active in his presidential campaigns. He died in 1996 at age 88."[24]

Because of its pervasiveness, sibling rivalry is a relatively straightforward phenomenon and one not too difficult to understand. But why did the two brothers remain close throughout their lives? And what was the nature of this close relationship? Clearly, one major source of cohesion in the relationship was the moral sense that both brothers had about assisting their parents and one another, especially when that assistance was needed. And throughout their lives, when assistance might be needed, Ronald would offer assistance to Neil, and Neil would reciprocate with his own offers of assistance to Ronald.

Perhaps this moral sense of helping one another was evidenced most by the numerous instances in which Ronald assisted Neil, and the fewer, yet significant, instances in which Neil assisted Ronald. Lou Cannon has noted that "[Nelle's] teachings also made an imprint. Ronald Reagan became his brother's keeper, cajoling him into quitting work and entering Eureka College and then finding him a job at radio station WOC in Davenport, Iowa, in the midst of the Depression. He also looked after his parents."[25] While Neil was at Eureka College and Ronald was working as a staff announcer for WOC, Ronald gave what would have been his 10 percent tithe to Neil for his support through school. Moreover, Ronald's assistance in helping Neil take the job at WOC in Davenport would provide the foundation for Neil's successful career in public relations.[26] Finally, after encouraging Neil and Bess to move to California, Ronald helped Neil attempt to break into the motion picture business by lining up a few minor roles for him. Neil was generally on the receiving end of the assistance provided by his brother in their early years, but Neil did manage to later assist Ronald with help in securing a contract as host of the television program *Death Valley Days*, and, of course, Neil provided significant assistance during his brother's gubernatorial campaign in 1966.

Overall, the Reagan brothers' relationship from their youth through their adult years resembled countless sibling relationships across America: It was competitive but close. It was, however, a unique relationship in Ronald Reagan's life, since it was competitive, close, and long term. It was a relationship characterized by mutual respect in spite of the considerable differences between the two brothers. Anne Edwards caught the quality of this relationship in her early biography of Ronald Reagan when she observed that after Moon and Bess had moved to California, "an irreversible pattern had set in between the brothers. Reagan [Ronald] held the dominant position. But it was not as though Moon walked in his shadow. Reagan respected Moon's opinion and like to have him near at hand."[27]

However, to respect an opinion is not always to agree with it, and Ronald Reagan stubbornly resisted for many years Moon's Republican views. And although both brothers would eventually leave the Democratic Party, Neil would make the break many years before Ronald did. To a significant degree, and not readily apparent to most observers, Neil's personal experience and reasons for making the break with his parents' political party would be important not only for himself but also for the political transformation of the future fortieth president of the United States.

threat it posed to U.S. security interests. He was particularly concerned now about Communist infiltration within American society, and he cooperated with the FBI to report on Communist activity in Hollywood. In this capacity, Neil Reagan advised his brother in 1946 to leave a Communist-infiltrated organization that Ronald had naively joined to promote New Deal and humanitarian principles. The organization, the Hollywood Independent Citizens Committee of the Arts, Sciences, and Professions (HICCASP, which boasted a membership comprising many Hollywood celebrities), initially appeared prestigious and honorable to Ronald Reagan. Neil Reagan, however, knew better and recalled warning his brother to "get out of that thing. There are people in there who can cause you real trouble. They're more than suspect on the part of the government, as to their connections that are not exactly American."[36] Anne Edwards later describes in her account how Ronald Reagan discovered on his own that HICCASP was infiltrated by Communists and Communist sympathizers and relayed this information to his brother. Neil's response? "I just looked at him and said, 'Junior, what do you suppose I've been talking about all these weeks and weeks and weeks?'"[37]

Lou Cannon supports the Edwards account. Cannon notes that Neil, "an anti-Communist conservative of long standing, had warned him repeatedly about the dangers of the Red menace, but Ronald Reagan argued with him whenever he mentioned the word 'Communist.'"[38] Ronald Reagan's stubbornness on policy matters has become legendary, but Neil Reagan experienced this trait of his brother's during their frequent debates and arguments over political philosophy. As a general rule, Ronald Reagan had to learn for himself; he was not easily persuaded, even by someone as close to him as his brother. Yet, out of this experience with HICCASP, Ronald Reagan undoubtedly placed greater trust in his brother's political judgment. This would not mean total agreement with Neil's political philosophy, but it did mean that Ronald Reagan would remember Neil's arguments about the Communist threat and that ultimately Neil would be vindicated on the matter of Communist infiltration into HICCASP. Political differences between the brothers would persist, but Neil Reagan's credibility grew out of this experience.

As Ronald Reagan continued to experience the tumultuous events of 1946 and 1947 described earlier in chapter 2, which radically altered his views about Communism, his conversations with his brother changed dramatically. By 1951, and perhaps earlier, he no longer argued with Neil about the Communist threat. Cannon notes that "never again would Reagan put up an argument when Neil told him that the Communists were behind something."[39]

However, arguments over politics persisted between the two brothers. Although Communism would not be a major source of disagreement during the

1950s, other political issues would divide the brothers. Nancy Reagan recalls, for instance, that after her marriage to Ronald in 1952, "Ronnie's brother, who was a conservative Republican, was always trying to convince him that the Democrats were all wrong. Moon and Ronnie had terrible arguments, and every time Moon and Bess came over to our house, the two brothers would get into a loud shouting match while Bess and I tried to get them off the subject. It's hard to imagine now, knowing Ronnie's personality, not to mention his political views, but it really did happen."[40] If these arguments were not about Communism, then what were they about? In all likelihood, these arguments were about the New Deal and the role of the federal government in domestic affairs. Ronald Reagan held to his New Deal beliefs well after his views had hardened against Communism, but this was not simply an intellectual or ideological attachment to the New Deal. After all, Ronald Reagan had viewed FDR as a hero for many years, and, of course, his father and mother had been strong Democrats and loyal supporters of FDR and the New Deal. Ronald Reagan had strong emotional attachments to FDR, the New Deal, and the Democratic Party.

However, just because Neil's arguments and debates with Ronald Reagan produced no palpable political conversion, we cannot conclude that Neil's influence was without effect. To the contrary, it is much more likely that Neil's influence had a more delayed effect on his brother. Clearly, Neil Reagan himself believed that his influence on his brother was delayed. Commenting on Neil and Ronald Reagan's arguments about the Communist threat, Lou Cannon noted, "[Ronald Reagan] believed, reasonably, that 'Red' was a charge that was hurled rather indiscriminately at Democrats and liberals. Neil Reagan, who years earlier had become a conservative Republican, disagreed, and the brothers would argue whenever Neil mentioned the word 'Communist' to Ronald. 'He would say right away quick, Oh, you're coming out with the Communist story,' Neil recalled. 'And then the occasion arose as a result of the strike [the Conference of Studio Unions in 1946] when these people began to hit him over the head, figuratively speaking. *And then, while I'm sure he [Ronald] would never admit it to me or to anyone else, some of the things I'd been saying to him began to soak in.*'"[41] It is unlikely that Neil's influence was without effect, but the effect was delayed and served to reinforce lessons about the Communist threat to freedom that Ronald Reagan had learned through his own experiences. And if Neil's arguments about the Communist threat had a more delayed than immediate effect on his brother, is this not also likely to be true when the two brothers argued about New Deal liberalism and an "encroaching federal government" a few years later? After all, Ronald Reagan's emotional ties to New Deal liberalism (because of

FDR and his parents) would presumably make it even more difficult for Neil to make this case than the earlier one about the Communist threat. And, as discussed in chapter 3, Ronald Reagan's experiences during his employment with General Electric would ultimately prove decisive in altering his views about the New Deal and the role of the federal government in domestic policy. Supporting this view, Nancy Reagan states in her memoir that, "as he [Ronald Reagan] traveled across the country for General Electric, Ronnie started seeing things differently. He became increasingly concerned about government interference in the free enterprise system—and also in the lives of individuals."[42] Clearly, learning about and responding to threats to American freedom was a gradual process for Ronald Reagan that took many years. But during this long process, the close and trusted voice of his brother, Neil, was most likely recalled from time to time, and that voice would clearly articulate warning messages about threats to American freedom.

A Close Friendship with George Murphy

As observed earlier, Ronald Reagan had many friendships, but few of them were close. Even fewer of his close friendships persisted over several decades. His friendship with screen actor George Murphy was one of those rare friendships—it was close, it was long, and it was characterized by mutual trust and respect. The friendship lasted for over half a century, until George Murphy's death in 1996.

Like many friendships, the one between Reagan and Murphy began as an acquaintance and gradually became closer over the years. Reagan moved to Hollywood in 1937, and the following year he became a member of the board of the Screen Actors Guild. In his early biography *Where's the Rest of Me?*, Reagan recalls that "in 1938, a novice in Hollywood, I suddenly found myself on the board of the SAG. The reason for it was not my fame nor fortune nor talents—but simply that the board had created a policy of a broad representation of all segments of the actors' world. They wanted day players, freelancers, extras (we represented them at the time), and stars alike. . . . One of the vacancies happened to fit my classification: new, young contract player. I accepted with awe and pleasure."[43] Reagan highly respected both the organization's purposes and its leadership. Again in his early 1965 biography, Reagan said, "Let me say here that I believe in the SAG with all my heart."[44] As Reagan took his seat on the board of the SAG in 1938, he would find himself working with the other board members, whom he highly respected, including George Murphy, who would become first vice president of the SAG just two years later in 1940. In 1944, Murphy was elected president of the SAG.[45]

Reagan and Murphy worked together on guild business for several years during the 1940s. After World War II, Reagan took a seat on the board of the SAG once again. In fact, "SAG president, George Murphy, suggested that the board ask him to return as a permanent member, and it was agreed."[46] During the next two to three years, Reagan and Murphy forged an even closer relationship as they worked together to oppose Communist infiltration throughout Hollywood and within the SAG itself. During this time frame, as we discovered in chapter 2, Reagan's views hardened against Communism, and Murphy played an influential role in this process. For instance, during the 1946 Conference of Studio Unions (CSU) strike, Reagan and Murphy were both on the SAG board and discovered evidence that strongly suggested Communist involvement in the strike. The friends worked together in successfully opposing the strike. The following year, Reagan was elected president, and Murphy was elected third vice president of the SAG. As president and past president of the guild, the two men testified together before the House Un-American Activities Committee on Communist infiltration in Hollywood and within the SAG. During his testimony, Reagan expressed his agreement with and complimented both George Murphy and Robert Montgomery for their earlier testimony on the matter.

George Murphy Turns Republican

As they began to get acquainted in the early 1940s, Reagan and Murphy no doubt quickly discovered that they had many things in common. They were both Irish, they were both athletes with a shared interest in football, they were both actors in Hollywood, they both had an interest in politics, and they both had been raised as Democrats in families fiercely loyal to the Democratic Party. In fact, commenting on Murphy's Democratic Party heritage, Anne Edwards writes, "Murphy's father had been a dedicated Democrat and a noted track coach who had prepared the U.S. team for the 1912 Olympics. From youth, Murphy's interest in politics had been as strong as his involvement in theater and films. A Democrat like his father, he arrived in Hollywood in 1934 after a successful career on Broadway as a duo dance act with his wife, Julie Johnson."[47] In his autobiography, George Murphy describes his early identification with the Democratic Party in a fashion quite similar to Ronald Reagan's experience. According to Murphy, "Until 1939, I was what you might call a dormant Democrat, faithful to the Party of Woodrow Wilson and Al Smith in a perfunctory way. Most of the Irish, particularly those on the Eastern Seaboard, were Democrats. It was largely a question of inheritance. Grandfather Long, for example, had been a Democratic member of the Michigan State Assembly. Most of the other members of my family and most of our friends considered themselves Democrats. So I was one too."[48]

However, only a few years after he and his wife arrived in Hollywood, George Murphy began to question the Democratic Party, President Roosevelt, and the president's New Deal agenda. As Murphy himself recalled, "I had become disenchanted with some of the excesses of the New Deal following the re-election of President Roosevelt in 1936."[49] Murphy identified a number of issues that concerned him at the time, but the major issue appeared to be the unprecedented growth and centralized control of the federal government in responding to the Great Depression. Recalling a conversation with Supreme Court Justice Frank Murphy (no relation to George Murphy) in 1940, George Murphy states that "[Justice Murphy] named some powerful persons who he felt were seeking to influence the White House in a wrong direction. He confirmed the fears that had been troubling me for some time—that there were powerful forces seeking to promote Socialism or some other form of centralized government."[50] Largely as a reaction against the New Deal, Murphy changed his party registration from Democrat to Republican in 1939. Murphy was thirty-seven years old when he became a Republican. His defection from the Democratic Party would be permanent. Like Neil Reagan, George Murphy's defection from the Democratic Party was largely a reaction *against* the New Deal. Both men developed their more hard-line views against Communism later when they would directly encounter Communist tactics and learn more about Communist ideology.

After his defection from the Democratic Party in 1939, Murphy went to work immediately for the Republican Party. In 1940, he helped to organize the Hollywood Republican Committee, which, in his words, was at least partly established to "combat the general belief that all Hollywood actors and writers belonged to the left wing."[51] The Committee also worked for the election of the Republican nominee for president, Wendell Willkie, who had also been a Democrat earlier. This small sample of defectors to the Republican Party does suggest, however, that the 1930s and 1940s were an unprecedented, turbulent, and uncertain period in which Americans were reexamining their many political beliefs and party loyalties. Beginning in 1943, George Murphy would help Ronald Reagan begin his own journey of reflection on these matters.

George Murphy's Influence

By the time George Murphy and Ronald Reagan got to know one another better (through their guild work and by working together on the film *This Is the Army*), Murphy had been in Hollywood for almost ten years and had become a well-established and successful movie star. Murphy was also the vice president of the Screen Actors Guild, head of the Hollywood Republican Committee, and an activist in the Republican Party. By contrast, Reagan had been recruited into the Hollywood Democratic Committee and, according to Edmund Morris, "had become an obsessive supporter of President Roosevelt's leftward swing."[52]

The differences between the two men were palpable to others on the film set. With hindsight, Edwards argues that "Murphy's influence during the making of *This Is the Army* cannot be discounted. Throughout the film they were constantly seen by others in 'animated debate.' And Reagan's already keen interest in the Screen Actors Guild intensified during this time."[53] Morris has a similar assessment in his biography. He observes that the "word from Warners was that he [Reagan] . . . had become an obsessive supporter of President Roosevelt's leftward swing, and his lunchtime dialogues with the conservative actor George Murphy verged on oratory."[54]

Despite their differences, the two men respected each other. The production of the film took about one year and provided considerable opportunity for Murphy to articulate his opposition to the New Deal and his growing concern with Communism. Undoubtedly, Murphy also conveyed to Reagan the specific reasons why he had left the Democratic Party for the Republican Party. During the one year it took to film *This Is the Army*, George Murphy and Ronald Reagan had enormous opportunity to air their political views with one another. However, in spite of their differences, they became friends. After the production of the film, the two would go their separate ways only to cross paths three years later. By 1946, Reagan had been discharged from the military and had resumed his acting career. He had also resumed his participation in the Screen Actors Guild by taking a seat on the board. George Murphy was on the board as well and had just completed a two-year term as president of the union. The two friends worked together over the next two years (1946 and 1947) to fight Communist infiltration in Hollywood. Clearly, as Reagan's views toward the Communists were hardening during this period, he must have recalled Murphy's earlier warnings about the Communists in 1943. Murphy's views about Communism had been vindicated— just as Neil Reagan's earlier warnings about Communist infiltration in Hollywood had been vindicated—and his credibility with Reagan was undoubtedly increased.

At this time, Reagan perceived that the immediate threat to freedom was Communism, not the encroaching federal government. By 1948, Reagan and Murphy would share similar views about the Communist threat to American freedom. Reagan, however, would hold to New Deal liberalism for almost ten more years. Nevertheless, when Reagan's views about the role of the federal government began to be altered during his General Electric years, he may have heard a second voice with that of his brother's, warning about the growing federal government and how the imbalance threatened American freedom. George Murphy, like Neil Reagan, had been right about Communism; perhaps Murphy was right about the federal government as well. Murphy's 1943 arguments against the expanded state may well have had a delayed effect on Reagan. In other words, Murphy's domestic policy arguments may have been more persuasive with Ronald Reagan fifteen years later than when he first articulated them during the filming of *This Is the Army*. After being planted, ideas, like seeds, may need some time to germinate and bear fruit. George Murphy seemed to be thinking along these lines when he observed in his 1970 autobiography, "Eventually, I am happy to report, Ronald Reagan discovered that I wasn't too far off the mark. Although he remained a liberal, he became increasingly anti-Communist. And, of course, as time went on he did decide that the Republican economic philosophy was more in keeping with his own. The rest is history still in the making."[55]

Later Family and Friends—1950s

After seeing each other regularly for over two years, Ronald Reagan and Nancy Davis were married on March 4, 1952. Reagan's marriage to Nancy Davis would graft him into a new set of family relationships and friends who would exercise influence on his political development during the 1950s. This network would principally include Reagan's new father-in-law, Loyal Davis, and a close friend of the Davis family, Barry Goldwater. Nancy Reagan was raised in a Republican home, and her father was an accomplished neurosurgeon with strong Republican beliefs. In addition, the Davis family had close ties with the Goldwaters of Phoenix, Arizona. To gauge this new Republican influence on Reagan's political development is not an easy task. In fact, the tendency of many who have attempted to do so has been to overestimate the influence of Nancy Reagan and her father, Loyal Davis, on Reagan's political development during the 1950s.

With only a superficial assessment, many journalists, writers, biographers, and others investigating Reagan's journey from Democrat to Republican have attributed inordinate influence to Nancy Reagan and Loyal Davis. In her memoir *My Turn*, Nancy Reagan notes that "Wanda McDaniel [a writer] also repeated a myth that I've heard *hundreds of times*: that my father was an extreme right-winger who was responsible for Ronnie's political shift from liberal to conservative. Or, in yet another article from that period, 'they fell in love, and Nancy converted him to her father's politics, and out popped Ronald Reagan, the right-winger.' Well, these stories hurt."[56] Reagan biographer Lou Cannon confirms the prevalence of these myths when he notes that "the perception of Nancy Reagan when I first met Reagan and started writing about him, which was in 1965, was that Nancy Reagan, with the help of her very conservative father, Loyal Davis, had converted this naïve and sort of wonderful wide-eyed liberal, Ronald Reagan, from his Democratic ways to the right-wing path and that Reagan had largely become a Goldwater Republican because of Nancy Reagan. The devil theory of Nancy Reagan in those days was that it was Nancy who had made Ronald Reagan a right-winger."[57]

These myths have greatly exaggerated Nancy Reagan's influence on her husband's political development. There is no evidence that Nancy Reagan exercised any significant influence on Ronald Reagan's political journey from Democrat to Republican during the 1950s. Rather, the evidence suggests that Nancy Reagan was first and foremost interested in Ronald Reagan and revealed little interest in political philosophy or public policy. By the time Ronald Reagan and Nancy Davis met in the fall of 1949, Reagan had largely developed his hard-line views toward Communism. On the other hand, Reagan still considered himself a New Deal liberal on domestic policy issues for several years after meeting Nancy. His views would begin changing on this element of his political philosophy during his employment with General Electric. His employment with GE began in 1954, two years after his marriage to Nancy, and Ronald Reagan would continue to think of himself as a New Deal liberal until 1955 or 1956. The General Electric experience would prove crucial to the development of his domestic policy views. Nancy Reagan recognized this when she wrote, "As he traveled across the country for General Electric, Ronnie started seeing things differently. He became increasingly concerned about government interference in the free enterprise system—and also in the lives of individuals. One day he came home from a speaking trip and told me he was starting to realize that the Democrats he had campaigned for in election years were responsible for the very things he was speaking out against between elections."[58]

Although Nancy Reagan assumed a very minor role in directly influencing Ronald Reagan's journey from Democrat to Republican during the 1950s, she may have assumed an indirect role by introducing her husband to her father, Loyal Davis, and her father's friend Barry Goldwater. Both Davis and Goldwater were Republicans who shared Reagan's hard-line views toward Communism but parted with Reagan's New Deal liberalism. Very much in the Republican tradition, Loyal Davis and Barry Goldwater opposed the New Deal and the expansion of federal government activism it represented. Rather, they favored a much more limited federal government and freer reign given to the domestic national economy and to the states. Davis and Goldwater would advance these views to Reagan in a variety of circumstances and locations after 1952. Their arguments would not convert Reagan, but their views would reinforce what Reagan learned while employed with General Electric.

Reagan met his new father-in-law shortly after he married Nancy in 1952. After their wedding at the Little Brown Church in San Fernando Valley, the Reagans spent a few days at the old Mission Inn in Riverside, California. They subsequently met with Nancy's father and mother in Phoenix, Arizona. The Davises had driven from Scottsdale and looked forward to their first meeting with their new son-in-law. Anne Edwards quotes Reagan as recalling, "Meeting . . . the doctor, wasn't the easiest moment I ever had."[59] However, as Edwards notes, "the two men got on well. In a very short time, they realized they had more than Nancy in common. Davis was a political man who had always lived a bit vicariously in the theatrical lives of Edith's [Davis] friends."[60] Dr. Davis had deep and focused interests. He has been described as an "honored and influential man of medicine and a heavy contributor to the Republican Party. Although the Davises were invited to almost all society fund-raising events, they were not included in the inner circle of Chicago's social register. Their close friends came mainly from the theater, the world of medicine and the Republican Party."[61] Reagan respected Dr. Davis, and their relationship grew closer over the years. As Anne Edwards notes, "Once Reagan signed with *General Electric Theater*, he and Nancy saw the Davises more often. The doctor and his son-in-law had a growing rapport. Reagan found it easy to stop in Arizona on his way home from a tour. He met and liked Davis's neighbor and good friend Senator Barry Goldwater. And the Davises traveled to the Coast to see the Reagans whenever they could."[62]

Reagan's visits to Davis and Goldwater undoubtedly included discussions about politics, but these discussions have not been precisely chronicled in Reagan's autobiographies and biographies. However, we do know that Reagan met Goldwater for the first time in 1952. It was also the same year that Goldwater won a U.S. Senate seat. As Reagan interacted with Davis and Goldwater from 1952 on, he was compelled to respect their high achievements and to grant them a substantial degree of credibility during their political discussions. The three men agreed about U.S. foreign policy and the threat of Communism to U.S. security interests. However, during the first

few years of Reagan's relationship with Davis and Goldwater, substantial disagreement occurred between Reagan and the two men over domestic policy.
More precisely, Reagan continued to defend the New Deal and its legacy,
while Davis and Goldwater naturally opposed it. Decades later, on September 9, 1986, when President Reagan telephoned Goldwater to honor him at
his retirement celebration from the U.S. Senate, Goldwater recalled these
early political differences when he told Reagan, "I remember one day when
you called me a Fascist SOB, but you have gotten over that."[63] These political debates with Davis and Goldwater no doubt reminded Reagan of the
countless arguments he had engaged in years earlier with Powell, Dart, Murphy, Neil Reagan, and others. And, like his earlier relationships, Reagan was
able to forge close friendships in spite of political differences. Nevertheless,
and in spite of his admiration and respect for Davis and Goldwater, Reagan
persisted in supporting the New Deal legacy, buttressed by his strong emotional ties to FDR. This would last, however, for only a few more years. Anne
Edwards has captured this time period and these relationships rather well
when she notes that "Reagan had met Goldwater just at the time of this great
victory [his U.S. Senate election]. He could not help but admire and identify
with the man. Goldwater was a great outdoorsman, an expert pilot, a confident speaker and a power in his own state. During the next twelve years, Reagan often came to Phoenix and saw Goldwater socially. A lot of the same
good-humored political arguments he had once had with . . . Dick Powell he
now had with Goldwater and Davis. By 1956, Reagan's friendship with Goldwater was close enough for the Reagans to christen their son (Ron, Jr.) with
the middle name 'Prescott,' one of Mrs. Goldwater's family's names."[64]

Reagan's friendship with Goldwater continued to grow throughout the
1950s and into the 1960s. When Goldwater launched his presidential campaign, Reagan was asked to be the cochairman of the campaign in California, and he accepted enthusiastically. As Reagan himself recalled, "When I
was asked to be the cochairman of Barry Goldwater's 1964 presidential campaign in California, I didn't hesitate a moment. I'd met Barry at the home of
Nancy's parents in Phoenix several years before and admired him greatly. His
book, *The Conscience of a Conservative*, contained a lot of the same points I'd
been making in my speeches and I strongly believed the country needed
him."[65] Of course, by 1964, Reagan's journey from Democrat to Republican
was complete, and his foreign *and* domestic policy positions agreed with
Goldwater's. Reagan and Goldwater, however, would grow more distant over
the years, and their friendship waned, particularly after the 1976 Republican
nominating campaign, when Goldwater endorsed incumbent President Gerald Ford rather than Reagan for the Republican presidential nomination.

Nevertheless, Goldwater and Davis both played important roles in Reagan's political development during the 1950s. They did not convert him into a Republican, but their credibility and their arguments, particularly those arguments about an overly intrusive federal government, no doubt created a few cracks in Reagan's New Deal armor. A new friend, a General Electric executive named Earl Dunckel, would enlarge those cracks.

In their book *Reagan: A Life in Letters*, Skinner, Anderson, and Anderson compiled over one thousand of Reagan's letters to family, friends, and colleagues written between 1922 and 1994. Their book provides ample evidence that Reagan was a prolific letter writer. The book also provides a list of twenty-four people referred to as "frequent correspondents," whom Reagan wrote to "so frequently as to merit special introduction."[66] Earl Dunckel is among those frequent correspondents designated in the book and is described as having "traveled with Reagan on the General Electric tours during 1954 and 1955. A self-described conservative, Dunckel debated politics with Reagan on their travels. Dunckel sent policy and political suggestions to Reagan regularly."[67]

Earl Dunckel first met Ronald and Nancy Reagan in August of 1954. Dunckel had a background as a newspaperman in Schenectady, New York, but had been asked to join *General Electric Theater*. He agreed to do so and was hired as a "communicator" and was subsequently asked to help manage *General Electric Theater* and assume responsibility for audience promotion. When Dunckel met Reagan in August 1954, it was with the knowledge that he would be working with and traveling with Reagan in promoting GE's new program and television series. At first, Dunckel was not looking forward to meeting Reagan, but he was pleasantly surprised to discover that Reagan "was as natural as anyone else you would ever meet. And whom I liked instantly."[68] The same month that Dunckel first met Reagan, he and another General Electric executive took Reagan on his first plant tour in Schenectady, New York. Reagan began hosting the television series the following month.

Dunckel and Reagan worked together visiting General Electric plants and local community groups across the country for about one year. Reagan had a fear of flying, so he and Dunckel traveled by rail. This obviously meant that the two men had plenty of time to talk—and argue—particularly about politics. They did this continuously. In fact, in a 1982 interview, Dunckel was asked, "When you were on a train going hither and thither and yon, was it usually some aspect of politics that you two would talk about?"[69] Dunckel responded, "We covered everything. I can't think of anything we didn't cover. Frequently, it got to that [politics]."[70] And, as fate would have it, Dunckel's

Republican political beliefs would inform his arguments against Reagan's New Deal liberalism. It is likely that Reagan had heard many if not most of Dunckel's arguments years earlier from his brother and from his Republican friends. He had also been hearing Republican arguments from his father-in-law, Loyal Davis, and from his friend Barry Goldwater for a couple of years before encountering Dunckel. Nevertheless, Reagan persisted in defending FDR and the New Deal.

Reagan's conversations and debates with Dunckel represented the culmination of Republican arguments that would assist Reagan in making his journey from Democrat to Republican. As Dunckel put it, "[Reagan's] politics were in the process of change. He had been a New Deal Democrat. He didn't like the way things were going, the trend of things. I was, am, and always will be an arch conservative. . . . I was drumbeating this [conservatism] at him all the time. Whenever he tried to defend New Dealism, or what was passing for it at the time, we would have some rather spirited arguments. I think this helped him to realize, as he put it later, that he didn't desert the Democratic Party; the Democratic Party deserted him."[71]

By 1956, Reagan had turned an important corner in his journey from Democrat to Republican. Sometime during 1955 or 1956, Reagan consciously decided that he was no longer a Democrat and would no longer defend the New Deal. He would maintain his Democratic Party registration for another six or seven years, but he would be a Democrat in name only; he realized that his values were closer to those of the Republican Party. As Dunckel later observed about Reagan's political development during his first year or so with GE, "During this time, through a juxtaposition of many things, he came to the realization that he was no longer a Democrat, that the gap had widened just too far to be bridged, that he was, he thought, following along the same path he'd always been on, but that the Democratic Party had veered off and left him. He found himself in so many things marching parallel with the Republicans."[72] However, Dunckel was astute enough to realize that when Reagan finally disassociated himself from the Democrats and the New Deal, it was part of a rather long journey. In 1982, Dunckel noted, "I think it was a combination of the fact that he had already begun the transfer process without consciously realizing it. I think our conversations may have had something to do with it, because I was prepared to discuss this at the drop of a hat, and would carry the hat."[73]

Dunckel's insight into Reagan's "transfer process" was sagacious. Clearly, Dunckel recognized that his role was part of a longer process in Reagan's journey from Democrat to Republican. Dunckel also recognized that a "combination" of factors contributed to Reagan's political evolution. The timing of

Dunckel's role was important. However, Dunckel's precise influence during debates with Reagan is difficult to measure and obviously subject to interpretation. Suffice it to say that Earl Dunckel, along with several other close friends and family members over the years, spoke to and argued with Reagan about many important political matters—they facilitated his journey from Democrat to Republican.

What Reagan Learned from Family and Friends

Reagan's journey from Democrat to Republican was long. Through the 1940s and 1950s, Reagan learned from his interactions with people, especially with credible and trusted family members and friends. Many of these people were Republicans who argued and debated with Reagan over many years. He no doubt heard many of the same arguments from his brother, his father-in-law, and his close Republican friends such as Dick Powell, Justin Dart, George Murphy, Barry Goldwater, and Earl Dunckel. They consistently and uniformly argued about the dangers of Communism and about the threats posed to individual freedom by increased centralized authority in the American federal system. They opposed the New Deal and the increased taxation and regulation it represented. Reagan listened to these arguments for years and yet remained unconvinced. That is, Reagan remained unconvinced until his circumstances changed and he began to directly experience the threat posed by Communism in Hollywood after World War II. His New Deal liberalism, however, persisted in spite of arguments to the contrary. Reagan's loyalty to FDR, and to his parents, impeded his move to the Republican Party. However, after a little over a year with General Electric, Reagan was ready to acknowledge that he was a Democrat in name only. He had not fully embraced the Republican Party yet, but he knew in his heart that he was no longer a Democrat. The party of his parents, the party of his hero FDR, the party of his youth, and the party of his early adulthood upheld beliefs and values that were contrary to his own.

Family and friends had played an important, yet only supportive, role in Reagan's journey. Clearly Reagan had not been converted by any one person's Republican arguments. However, the cumulative effect of many credible and trusted family members and friends who advanced the same or similar arguments had some influence, even if it was not immediate. Those arguments had to wait for the appropriate time, and the appropriate time came when Reagan encountered circumstances in the 1940s and 1950s that seriously challenged his liberal views. At that time, he no doubt remembered his close Republican family members and friends and the spirited arguments they had advanced earlier, but it was not just the substantive arguments that mattered to Reagan. Some Republican family members and friends, most notably Neil Reagan and George Murphy, had at one time been Democrats themselves. They would share with Reagan their own experience of leaving one party and identifying with another. Consequently, their arguments about why they left the Democrat Party for the Republican Party were unique and were hardly inconsequential.

Finally, the Republican family members and friends who frequently engaged Reagan in political debate during the 1940s and 1950s remembered that it was often animated and spirited. This theme is an important thread that runs through many of Reagan's interactions with his family and friends during his political journey. Yet with convictions on both sides of the debate running so strong, there is no evidence that Reagan was mean spirited or that he resorted to personal attacks against Republicans. Actually, the evidence is quite the contrary. In spite of Reagan's differences with his Republican family members and friends, he valued and respected each one. Their relationships actually grew closer over the years. By maintaining self-discipline and a steady focus on the issues during contentious political discourse, Reagan demonstrated the value of civility during partisan debate. His later ability as president to work effectively with political adversaries rather than attacking them was an ability that was clearly evident before his political career was even launched in the 1960s. Reagan's civility in contentious debates with Republicans during the 1940s and 1950s was similarly reflected in his debates with Democrats during his presidency in the 1980s.

Notes

1. Nancy Reagan, My Turn: The Memoirs of Nancy Reagan (New York: Random House, 1989), 106.

2. Ronald Reagan and Richard Hubler, Where's the Rest of Me? (New York: Dell, 1965), 163.

3. Garry Wills, Reagan's America (New York: Doubleday, 1987), 137.

4. Ronald Reagan and Richard Hubler, Where's the Rest of Me? 100.

5. Ibid., 153.

6. Anne Edwards, Early Reagan (New York: William Morrow, 1987), 229.

7. Ibid., 246.

8. Ibid., 229–30.

9. Thomas C. Hayes, "Close Reagan Business Friends," New York Times, October 30, 1980, D1.

10. Anne Edwards, Early Reagan, 16.

11. Ibid., 197.

12. Ibid.

13. Ibid.

14. Ibid., 294.

15. Joanne Drake, Office of Ronald Reagan, "Statement for Immediate Release: Death of Neil Reagan on December 11, 1996," statement date of December 12, 1996, reproduced at the Ronald Reagan Presidential Library.

16. Ibid.

17. Anne Edwards, *Early Reagan*, 35.

18. Lou Cannon, *Reagan* (New York: G. P. Putnam's Sons, 1982), 28.

19. Garry Wills, *Reagan's America*, 28.

20. Ibid., 29.

21. Ibid.

22. Ibid.

23. Anne Edwards, *Early Reagan*, 55.

24. Kiron Skinner, Annelise Anderson, and Martin Anderson, eds., *Reagan: A Life in Letters* (New York: Free Press, 2003), 43.

25. Lou Cannon, *President Reagan: The Role of a Lifetime* (New York: Public Affairs, 2000), 176.

26. William Pemberton, *Exit with Honor: The Life and Presidency of Ronald Reagan* (New York: M. E. Sharpe, 1997), 15.

27. Anne Edwards, *Early Reagan*, 201.

28. Ibid., 183.

29. Ibid., 246.

30. Lou Cannon, *Governor Reagan: His Rise to Power* (New York: Public Affairs, 2003), 41.

31. Ibid.

32. Garry Wills, *Reagan's America*, 61–62.

33. Ronald Reagan, *An American Life*, 105.

34. *Los Angeles Times*, "Republican Convention—Kansas City," August 18, 1976, reproduced at the Ronald Reagan Presidential Library.

35. Anne Edwards, *Early Reagan*, 254.

36. Ibid., 303.

37. Ibid., 304.

38. Lou Cannon, *President Reagan: The Role of a Lifetime*, 243.

39. Lou Cannon, *Reagan*, 87.

40. Nancy Reagan, *My Turn: The Memoirs of Nancy Reagan*, 129.

41. Lou Cannon, *Governor Reagan: His Rise to Power*, 93, emphasis added.

42. Nancy Reagan, *My Turn: The Memoirs of Nancy Reagan*, 129.

43. Ronald Reagan and Richard Hubler, *Where's the Rest of Me?* 153.

44. Ibid.

45. George Murphy, *Say . . . Didn't You Used to Be George Murphy?* (New York: Bartholomew House, 1970), 219.

46. Anne Edwards, *Early Reagan*, 300.

47. Anne Edwards, *Early Reagan*, 273.

48. George Murphy, *Say . . . Didn't You Used to Be George Murphy?* 259.

49. Ibid.

50. Ibid., 262.

51. Ibid., 264.

52. Edmund Morris, *Dutch* (New York: Random House, 1999), 205.

53. Ibid.

54. Ibid.

55. George Murphy, *Say . . . Didn't You Used to Be George Murphy?* 280.

56. Nancy Reagan, *My Turn: The Memoirs of Nancy Reagan*, 37, emphasis added.

57. Lou Cannon, "Discussant," in *Ronald Reagan's America*, ed. Eric Schmertz, Natalie Datlof, and Alexej Ugrinsky (Westport, CT: Greenwood Press, 1997), 2:674.

58. Nancy Reagan, *My Turn: The Memoirs of Nancy Reagan*, 129.

59. Anne Edwards, *Early Reagan*, 431.

60. Ibid.

61. Ibid., 388.

62. Ibid., 458.

63. Barry Goldwater, "Remarks by Telephone to Senator Barry Goldwater." The Public Papers of President Ronald W. Reagan. Ronald Reagan Presidential Library. http://www.reagan.utexas.edu/archives/speeches/1986/090986f.htm (accessed 2 February 2006).

64. Anne Edwards, *Early Reagan*, 482–83.

65. Ronald Reagan, *An American Life*, 138–39.

66. Kiron Skinner, Annelise Anderson, and Martin Anderson, eds., *Reagan: A Life in Letters*, xvii.

67. Ibid., xviii.

68. Earl B. Dunckel, "Ronald Reagan and the General Electric Theater, 1954–1955," an oral history conducted in 1982 by Gabrielle Morris, Regional Oral History Office, the Bancroft Library, University of California, 1982, 6.

69. Ibid., 23.

70. Ibid.

71. Ibid., 15.

72. Ibid., 22.

73. Ibid., 23.

CHAPTER FIVE

Intellectuals

Like many Americans, Ronald Reagan was an intelligent and practical man who learned primarily from his life experiences. He was not an intellectual who elevated the value of abstract thought and reasoning in the learning process, the way college professors, lawyers, journalists, and others do. Reagan did, however, attach significant value to the ideas of selected intellectuals, and he relied on these ideas to reinforce the conclusions he had come to through his own experiences with Communism and the federal government during the 1940s and 1950s. In this respect, intellectual influences played an important but largely secondary role in Reagan's political development.

Unfortunately, some intellectuals might be incredulous that Reagan was subject to any intellectual influence at all during his journey from Democrat to Republican. It is a destructive myth perpetuated by many, particularly by intellectuals, that Reagan was unintelligent and that he was therefore manipulated by his "handlers." Dinesh D'Souza, for instance, notes that "he was, in diplomat Clark Clifford's view, an amiable dunce. Columnist Michael Kinsley charged that Reagan was not terribly bright and was therefore not up to the most important job in the world. Robert Wright of the *New Republic* pronounced him virtually brain-dead. Frances FitzGerald wrote that Reagan knew little more than what was written on the three-by-five cards his advisers handed him. Writing in *Harper's*, Nicholas von Hoffman confessed that it was 'humiliating to think of this unlettered, self-assured bumpkin being our president.'"[1] The academic world has been hardly less critical of Reagan's intelligence, as epitomized by presidential scholar Fred Greenstein's observation that Reagan had "cognitive limitations." If these intellectuals are accurate in their assessment of Reagan's intelligence, it is hard to see how any intellectual influence could guide his thinking at all. Most assuredly, however, these assessments are highly inaccurate. They do a disservice to Reagan and the nation by perpetuating an unfounded myth.

Reagan's Intellect

By contrast, more accurate assessments of Reagan's intellect, and therefore of his capacity to be influenced by certain intellectuals, have been provided by a variety of distinguished scholars, including political scientist Hugh Heclo. In his article "Ronald Reagan and the American Public Philosophy," Heclo takes issue with the more conventional academic assessment of Reagan's capacity for political thought by noting that "for almost two generations, Reagan's more intellectually sophisticated critics in mainstream academia—and there have been a great many—have found it absurd to characterize Ronald Reagan as any sort of thinker, much less a figure in public philosophy. However, that is exactly what he was. To be sure, Ronald Reagan did not engage the world of ideas in the intellectually sophisticated, abstract way of which academics approve. He did so as a public man seeking political power in the name of certain ideas."[2] Heclo affirms that "Reagan was a man of ideas born out of life experiences, even though he was not a thinker's idea of a thinker."[3]

Other scholars have drawn similar conclusions. In his book *The Age of Reagan: The Fall of the Old Liberal Order, 1964–1980*, Steven Hayward argues that "if Reagan wasn't the most intelligent or intellectual politician of his time, he instinctively grasped not only the power of ideas, but also the crucial relationship of ideas to power. It is a great injustice to suggest that Reagan got his ideas secondhand or in a superficial way."[4] Peter Wallison, a former Treasury Department counsel during the Reagan administration, said much the same thing in his book *Ronald Reagan: The Power of Conviction and the Success of His Presidency*. Wallison, a Harvard Law School graduate, argues that "Reagan's weapon in this effort [to advance his agenda] was not the political power he held as president. It was the ideas he would put before the American people."[5]

Recent scholarship by a top domestic adviser to Reagan helps dispel the myth of Reagan as an amiable dunce with cognitive limitations. Martin Anderson, an intellectual himself with a PhD in economics and a coveted position at the Hoover Institution at Stanford University, notes that Nancy Reagan disclosed in an interview, "I can see him sitting at his desk writing, which he seemed to do all the time. Often he'd take a long shower because he said that was where he got a lot of his thoughts. He'd stand in the shower and think about what he wanted to write. And then, when he got out, he'd sit down and write. . . . Nobody thought that he ever read anything either—but he was a voracious reader. I don't ever remember Ronnie sitting and watching television. I really don't. I just don't. When I picture those days, it's him sitting behind that desk in the bedroom, working."[6] And, indeed, Reagan did write a lot; we are just now discovering what a prolific writer he was through two very important books edited by Martin Anderson and two colleagues.

Anderson's books contain an enormous amount of Reagan's original writing on a variety of subjects. The first book, *Reagan, In His Own Hand* (2001), is a collection of about 670 original handwritten drafts of policy essays written by Reagan for radio broadcast from 1975 to 1979. There was no ghostwriter. In fact, the book includes photocopies of Reagan's original drafts, thus the title: *In His Own Hand.* The essays reveal an alert, active, and informed mind presenting arguments buttressed with evidence on Reagan's philosophy of government, foreign policy, domestic and economic policy, and other topics. George Shultz, secretary of state under Reagan, wrote the foreward to the book and observed that the essays were "written to be listened to, to be broadcast once into the air, and then to disappear. But luckily, about 670 of the original handwritten drafts were saved, hidden away for over 20 years. Now they have been found and they force us to reflect on the light they shed on the mind and the capability of the man, Ronald Reagan."[7]

The second Anderson book, *Reagan, A Life in Letters* (2003), is a collection of over a thousand letters to family, friends, colleagues, and others written during a seventy-two-year period, 1922 to 1994. As Anderson notes, "Reagan revealed himself—his beliefs, his values, his character, and his policies—through these private letters."[8] Taken together, the two books reveal a man who is thoughtful, knowledgeable, and coherent in his beliefs. The letters provide direct evidence that clearly contradicts the conventional wisdom concerning Reagan's intellectual capacity. People who review and evaluate the two books will likely agree with Shultz that, "well, maybe he was a lot smarter than most people thought."[9] And, as Lou Cannon once noted, "[George] Will and others who knew Reagan personally or who dealt with him over a long period of time usually concluded that he was smarter, maybe much smarter, than he seemed on the surface."[10]

Shultz, who saw Reagan up close in a variety of situations, including negotiations with the Soviets over nuclear arms reductions, identified a key element in Reagan's intelligence. Shultz observed that Reagan had a "social" intelligence that served him and America well. Shultz noted, "I could see this human sensitivity in the way Ronald Reagan handled himself. Whenever he met a head of government for the first time, his clear intent was less to develop the talking points and more to get a feeling for what kind of person this was. . . . The point is that Ronald Reagan had a capacity to sit down and engage with someone and in the process make a judgment about the character of the individual sitting opposite him."[11] This talent served Reagan particularly well in his talks with Mikhail Gorbachev. Clearly this talent is a form of intelligence that is not conventionally recognized by intelligence tests or guaranteed by formal education. Yet Reagan's critics have seldom recognized this type of intelligence and have insisted instead that we evaluate Reagan's intellectual capacity strictly and narrowly in the analytical sense.

However, Peter Wallison asks, "What is intelligence? Anyone who has kept his eyes open to the world around him knows that there are many kinds of skills that we consider intelligence—the good test taker's ability to memorize and repeat facts and figures; the architect's ability to conceptualize space; the philosopher or mathematician's ability to reason symbolically; the lawyer's ability to recognize fact patterns in applying principles to facts; a doctor's ability to make a diagnosis. The radio addresses [*Reagan, In His Own Hand*] show that Reagan possessed a rare and powerful intelligence—the ability to understand and summarize complex material in clear and understandable form."[12]

Reagan biographer Lou Cannon has made a similar observation. Cannon struggled for years trying to understand the nature of Reagan's intelligence. Cannon knew Reagan was intelligent in an unconventional sense, yet he could not quite explain or describe the nature of his intelligence. Cannon then discovered Harvard psychologist Howard Gardner's book, *Frames of Mind: The Theory of Multiple Intelligences*, which allowed Cannon to understand Reagan's intelligence. Gardner's theory that there are multiple intelligences, including interpersonal and language intelligences, was the basis for Cannon's remark that "Gardner's analysis of the way Reagan functions intellectually produced in me the sense of discovery that a scientist or a detective must feel when a gigantic mystery abruptly becomes comprehensible."[13] Cannon's analysis included the conclusion that "Reagan ranks high in a form of intelligence [called] 'interpersonal' [or social], high in 'bodily-kinesthetic intelligence,' high in an aspect of 'language intelligence' and low in the 'logical-mathematical intelligence' [or analytical] at which lawyers and professors usually excel."[14] Is it surprising, then, that so many intellectuals have criticized Reagan's intellect? Many have not only disagreed with his political philosophy and public policies but have not understood his mind.

Another distinguishing element in Reagan's intellect was its proclivity to rely less on analysis and more on narration in comprehending reality. Howard Gardner once observed that "[Reagan] makes sense of the world narratively."[15] This simply means that Reagan often relied on stories and anecdotes to interpret reality. This is uncommon in American presidents, largely because so many have had legal or military backgrounds that place a premium on analysis. However, uncommon intelligence does not imply inferior intelligence. On the contrary, one could argue that Reagan's narrative intelligence—important to effective political leadership—was more greatly needed to inspire Americans after their "malaise" of the 1970s.

Reagan's narrative outlook on reality—that is, his understanding of reality primarily in terms of a story or script—was fundamental to Reagan's unique ability to articulate a story about America to Americans in the latter half of the twentieth century. According to Howard Gardner, this talent is fundamental to highly effective leadership. In his highly acclaimed book *Leading Minds: An Anatomy of Leadership*, Gardner examines eleven case studies on the psychology of leadership and makes a very important discovery: He finds that effective leaders articulate stories to their followers—and the *most* effective leaders articulate stories of identity. Gardner argues that "stories speak to both parts of the human mind—its reason and emotion. And [he] suggests, further, that it is *stories of identity*—narratives that help individuals think about and feel who they are, where they come from, and where they are headed—that constitute the single most powerful weapon in the leader's literary arsenal."[16] Reagan's effectiveness in conveying to the American people a sense of their historical identity at a time when America was arguably in an identity crisis was truly a crucial element in his leadership. And although many people, including Reagan's critics, have recognized his role as the "Great Communicator," fewer people have realized that his effectiveness as a communicator was fundamentally linked to his narrative intelligence.

Historical Context and Intellectual Influences

In his review of the book *Reagan*, by Lou Cannon, John Judis astutely observed in 1983, "Reagan cannot be understood outside the context of the conservative movement. It is as if one tried to write a biography of French president François Mitterrand and left out his experiences in the French Socialist Party."[17] Judis had criticized Cannon's early book on Reagan for ignoring the post–World War II conservative movement and its influence on

Ronald Reagan's political development. In the review, Judis wrote that "according to Cannon, Reagan was drawn to the right primarily through his 1954–62 experiences as a traveling spokesman for G.E. . . . [but] Cannon consistently understates or ignores Reagan's conservative commitments. His [Cannon's] account of the G.E. years is blank on Reagan's reading or political associations during that period."[18] Lou Cannon's subsequent biographies on Reagan have responded to the Judis critique and do include more coverage on Reagan's reading and intellectual development apart from his GE experiences. However, the early Cannon omission is a common one, particularly for those predisposed to think that Reagan rarely read anything, that he was passive and intellectually lazy, and that he was easily manipulated by wealthy friends. Presidential scholars Fred Greenstein and James David Barber similarly neglected an assessment of the intellectual influences on Reagan and focused inordinately on his experience in Hollywood with Communism and on his later General Electric employment in explaining his political transformation.[19]

However, the evidence strongly suggests that although Reagan was not an intellectual, and although his reading of intellectuals was not a primary influence on his political development, his reading of certain intellectual works during the late 1940s and through the 1950s nevertheless was important and reinforced his convictions that American freedom was threatened by both Communism and an encroaching and overly intrusive federal government.

Historical Context

It is notable that Ronald Reagan learned about threats to American freedom at a time when many intellectuals in the United States clearly did not discern threats from either Communism or the American federal bureaucracy. Actually, the situation was quite the contrary. Most American intellectuals were liberals at the time and believed that Communism posed little if any threat to the United States. Moreover, the New Deal and its legacy promised liberation for the individual, not repression by the state. The dominance of this ideological paradigm was palpable in American society. As Robert Nisbet has observed, "*Liberalism reigned supreme* virtually unchallenged as a national philosophy through the 1950s. . . . Liberalism was everywhere, in all spheres and walks, and at all levels, of American life throughout the 1950s."[20] Within this context, Reagan's postwar political development challenged the dominant public philosophy of liberalism. However, Reagan was not alone. Others, including a significant array of intellectuals, began raising their voices and pens against perceived foreign and domestic threats to American freedom.

What has been described as a conservative intellectual renaissance began to emerge during the 1950s and gathered significant strength over the next few decades. Martin Anderson has described this "conservative ascendancy as the logical outgrowth of policy ideas and political forces set in motion during the 1950s and 1960s, ideas and forces that gathered strength and speed during the 1970s, then achieved political power during the 1980s, and promise to dominate national policy in the United States for the remainder of the twentieth century."[21] Reagan would discover compatible thinking with many conservative intellectuals who warned of threats to American freedom during the 1950s. These intellectuals, many of whom had once been Communists or liberals themselves, attempted to make their case from three vantage points.

In his classic book *The Conservative Intellectual Movement in America Since 1945*, George Nash identifies three veins of the conservative intellectual movement and surveys the literature in each vein in substantial detail. William Rusher has described Nash's work as "comprehensive . . . the definitive study of this subject."[22] And in this acclaimed book, Nash informs us that "gradually during the first postwar decade these [conservative] voices multiplied, acquired an audience, and began to generate an intellectual movement. In the beginning one finds not one right-wing renaissance but three, the subjects of the first several chapters of this book."[23]

Nash's first vein of conservatism consisted of the classical liberals and economic libertarians who "resisted the threat of the ever expanding State to liberty, private enterprise, and individualism."[24] The thinkers in this genre were intellectuals who attacked the presuppositions of statist or socialist political philosophy. The Austrian economists, such as Friedrich A. Hayek and Ludwig von Mises, and libertarian intellectuals, such as Frank Chodorov, Henry Hazlitt, Leonard Read, John Chamberlain, and others, mounted an offensive against centralized economic planning—including the New Deal legacy.

The second vein of the movement emerged independently of the first. Thinkers in this second genre were often referred to as the "traditionalists." The traditionalists rejected the social relativism of the day and attempted to reassert a transcendent moral order as expressed through traditional religious beliefs and classical philosophy. Traditionalist thinkers included Russell Kirk, Richard Weaver, Peter Viereck, and Robert Nisbet. Leo Strauss and his students, the so-called Straussian political philosophers, were also considered part of this traditionalistic school of thought.

Finally, Nash's third vein of conservatism consisted of intellectuals who were "militant, evangelistic anti-Communists."[25] Many of the intellectuals in this last genre were "former men of the Left [who] brought to the postwar Right a profound conviction that the West was engaged in a titanic struggle with an implacable adversary—Communism—which sought nothing less than conquest of the world."[26] Their numbers "included Whittaker Chambers, James Burnham, Frank Meyer, and many more."[27]

These and many other intellectuals produced a plethora of books and articles advancing their conservative views during the late 1940s and throughout the 1950s. Their publications provided the intellectual firepower for a nascent conservative movement that otherwise would not have gathered strength during the 1950s. A small sampling includes Friedrich Hayek's *The Road to Serfdom* (1944), Richard Weaver's *Ideas Have Consequences* (1948), James Burnham's *The Coming Defeat of Communism* (1950), Whittaker Chambers's *Witness* (1952), and Russell Kirk's *The Conservative Mind* (1953). Also published during the 1950 to 1953 time frame were Eric Voegelin's *The New Science of Politics*, Leo Strauss's *Natural Right and History*, and William F. Buckley's *God and Man at Yale*.[28] Tocqueville and Burke were rediscovered during the 1950s. Conservative journals also emerged and experienced a renaissance. For instance, *Human Events*, established in 1944, increased its subscriptions, while new conservative journals such as William F. Buckley's *National Review*, which emerged in 1955, helped to fuse together articles from all three veins of conservatism: the libertarian, traditionalist, and anti-Communist perspectives. Just two years later, in 1957, Russell Kirk's quarterly journal titled *Modern Age: A Conservative Review* appeared. The quarterly emphasized traditionalist themes, especially themes associated with the political thought of Edmund Burke.

Beyond book publications and journals, there were additional contributions to the conservative renaissance. Robert Nisbet notes that "by the end of the 1950s a conservative culture and network were visible in this country, still small but growing. There were a few journals, the most important of which was *National Review* founded earlier in the decade by Buckley. Conservative clubs, primarily intellectual, sprang up in the suburbs across the country and also, more important, on college campuses. Visiting lecturers with conservative credentials became more common even on large university campuses, sponsored for the most part by student groups. Conservative institutes and foundations began to show themselves. The American Enterprise Institute and the Hoover Institution had been founded earlier but this was the decade in which they began to show life and start the growth that would make them models for other conservative institutes in the 1960s and 1970s."[29]

During this renaissance of conservative intellectual thought during the 1950s, Ronald Reagan was undergoing his own political development. Reagan would eventually find an intellectual kinship with many of these intellectuals. But to what degree did this renaissance of conservative political thought influence Reagan's journey from Democrat to Republican?

Intellectual Influences

Although intellectual influences can come from a wide array of sources, I am principally concerned with Ronald Reagan's reading of the works of various intellectuals and their influence on Reagan's political development during the 1950s. Unfortunately, a myth persists that Reagan never read much during his lifetime. The evidence, however, is to the contrary. Even as a child, Reagan had an unusual appetite for books. In the first year of his presidency, Reagan wrote a letter responding to a question from a Dixon resident about the Dixon Public Library when Reagan was a child. The Dixon resident, Miss Helen Miller, had asked Reagan "what the Dixon Library meant to him." Reagan responded with a letter dated September 3, 1981, in which he discussed not only his love for the Dixon Library but his lifelong love of reading as well. Reagan wrote, "I can barely remember a time in my life when I didn't know how to read. . . . The joy of reading has always been with me. Indeed, I can't think of greater torture than being isolated in a guest room or a hotel room without something to read."[30] Reagan then wrote about his favorite authors and books during childhood and concluded the letter by noting that "the [Dixon] library was really my house of magic. Now and then I would take a foray upstairs to the Indian museum where I was fascinated by the artifacts and (at that time) the full length birch bark canoe. But mainly it was the books, and I can assure you the love of books still stays with me. I now have a library of my own and am very proud of it. But as I say—it all started there in my house of magic—the Dixon Public Library. Thank you for your kind letter and best regards."[31] Reagan biographer Lou Cannon attests to the former president's lifelong reading habit and observes, "One reason that outsiders underestimated the extent of Reagan's reading was that he often forgot the titles of books, even books he quoted. He also seemed to have a reader's conceit that books were secret, personal treasures: He never cared, as far as I could tell, if anyone else knew that he was a reader."[32]

Although Reagan's appetite for reading persisted into his adult years, the nature of his reading obviously changed. In his compilation of the Reagan letters, Martin Anderson notes that "as an adult Reagan read a wide range of books, newspapers, and magazines. . . . The library at Reagan's ranch included many books on the American West, California's natural and political history, and horse training and breeding."[33] The library also included works on history, politics, economics, and leadership.[34] Some might falsely conclude that Reagan began reading articles and books on these academic subjects sometime after being elected governor of California. However, Reagan developed this reading interest much earlier. After all, he had majored in economics and sociology at Eureka College, and he sustained an interest in those disciplines throughout his adult years. His reading, particularly during the late 1940s and throughout the 1950s, reflected his increased interest in the twin threats to American freedom: Soviet Communism and a growing domestic federal governmental bureaucracy. Reagan's reading habits during these dynamic years included many different articles and books that scholars and biographers have often overlooked. On the whole, these articles and books did not by themselves transform Reagan's political outlook, but they did convince him that the practical truths he had discovered through his own experience had intellectual credibility as well.

It is well established that Reagan read conservative journals and magazines quite regularly during the 1950s. These periodicals included *Human Events*, *National Review*, and *Reader's Digest*.[35] Martin Anderson has noted that Reagan read the *National Review* "regularly from its founding [1955] through his presidency."[36] Reagan biographer Lee Edwards has observed that Reagan read *Human Events* before he began reading *National Review* but that both periodicals, and the *Reader's Digest*, were important sources for Reagan's General Electric speeches. Those speeches culminated in his 1964 "Time for Choosing" address for Barry Goldwater.[37] As Reagan scholar Ted McAllister has observed, these articles "shaped his understanding and articulation of the issues."[38] Fortunately for Reagan, he was exposed to articles drawn from all three veins of conservative thought—libertarian, traditionalist, and anti-Communist—through his long-term reading of *National Review*. For instance, in contrast to the libertarian *Freeman* and Russell Kirk's *Modern Age*, which emphasized the traditionalist vein of conservative intellectual thought, Buckley's *National Review* contained a good representation of articles across the emerging factions of conservatism. As George Nash has observed, "Buckley's success in welding a coalition was substantial. New conservatives, libertarians, and anti-Communists were represented on the masthead and readily gained access to the pages of the magazine."[39] The important roles played by both Buckley and Frank Meyer in tying together the uneasy alliance of libertarian, traditionalist, and anti-Communist strands of intellectual thought under the banner of conservatism were nothing short of remarkable. In fact, it has been noted that Buckley's and Meyer's contributions in "fusing" these veins of intellectual thought under the broader rubric of political conservatism "allowed Barry Goldwater, Ronald Reagan, and innumerable other politicians to embrace free-market capitalism, traditional morality, and anti-Communism simultaneously."[40] However, before Reagan was elected to any public office, *National Review*'s synthesis of diverse articles during the 1950s helped prepare the intellectual groundwork for Reagan's political development.

Beyond his reading of *National Review*, *Human Events*, *Reader's Digest*, and other journals and magazines during the 1950s, Reagan also read conservative books. Scholars and biographers of Reagan have often found it difficult to identify and describe the various books that influenced his thinking during this period. It seems apparent, however, that Reagan's reading within the three veins of the nascent conservative intellectual movement of the 1950s favored the libertarian and anti-Communist veins over the traditionalist literature. This makes sense when we remember the historical context. The immediate threats to American freedom seemed to Reagan to be the Communist threat and the growing domestic federal governmental bureaucracy. Most of the social issues that would mobilize the so-called Religious Right would not emerge for another decade or two. Consequently, the traditionalist literature at the time would likely seem less compelling not only to Reagan but also to millions of Americans. Perhaps, too, the traditionalist literature was viewed as a bit too esoteric and philosophical for Reagan's tastes; the libertarian and anti-Communist literature had a practical bent that would appeal to Reagan.

In the anti-Communist genre of books, Reagan read two books in the late 1940s that contained a similar theme: the author's disillusionment with and repudiation of Communism. Reagan read the books at a time when growing numbers of Communists were turning their backs on Communism. In his book *Reagan's War*, Peter Schweizer notes that "Reagan had read [Arthur] Koestler's *Darkness at Noon* and a 1949 book called *The God That Failed*, which included chapters by former high-profile Communists who had renounced their past."[41] It is hard to know precisely how the books may have influenced Reagan's thinking, but in 1949, Reagan and five others wrote a letter titled "You Too Can Be Free Men Again," published in the *Saturday Evening Post*, which was an "offer of help to those who wanted to switch sides in the cold war divide."[42] Reagan's reading of these two books, combined with his personal knowledge of ex-Communists who broke away from the party, may well have prompted him to reach out with assistance to former Communists. As Schweizer has noted, "Reagan had great respect for those who were baring their souls and switching sides."[43]

However, the book in the anti-Communist genre that had the greatest influence on Reagan during the 1950s was clearly *Witness* by Whittaker Chambers. A powerful book written by a former Communist who described his disillusionment with and repudiation of Communism, *Witness* had a profound influence on millions throughout the world, including Reagan. In fact, many would agree with William Rusher, author of *The Rise of the Right*, that "there is little doubt that Hayek's *The Road to Serfdom*, Kirk's *The Conservative Mind*, and Chambers's *Witness* were the three most powerful philosophical contributions to the conservative movement that was stirring intellectually in the early 1950s."[44]

Reagan read *Witness* shortly after its publication in 1952, and he probably read a condensed version of Friedrich Hayek's *The Road to Serfdom* even earlier. *Witness* would reinforce Reagan's anti-Communist views, and *The Road to Serfdom* would support his emerging views about the threat to freedom due to an encroaching federal bureaucracy. Reagan would clearly acknowledge his own intellectual debt to these two great thinkers.

Witness

In his book *The Conservative Intellectual Movement in America*, George Nash recognizes the monumental impact of Chambers's *Witness* on American society and on the conservative movement in America after World War II. Nash observes that *Witness* was "recognized at once as one of the most significant autobiographies of the twentieth century, [and] the book immediately became a best-seller."[45] Published in 1952, *Witness* was Whittaker Chambers's personal story about his repudiation of his Communist beliefs and his conversion to Christianity. The book, however, was much more than an autobiography that focused on Chambers's journey to religious faith. The book was more generally a narrative that identified the conflict between the United States and the Soviet Union as fundamentally a spiritual conflict between two distinctive faiths: faith in God versus faith in man. The conflict between the American and Soviet political systems was secondary or derivative of the fundamental difference in worldviews presented by the two clashing spiritual ideologies.

Paul Kengor has captured the core of *Witness* in his book *God and Ronald Reagan: A Spiritual Life*. In his book, Kengor recognizes that "of all the writers who had an impact on Reagan, the most influential was the former KGB operative turned anti-Communist crusader Whittaker Chambers. No serious attempt to craft a spiritual biography of Reagan can fail to draw upon the spiritual autobiography that Chambers published in 1952—a volume that dwelt particularly on the author's firsthand account of the conflict between God and Communism. Indeed, among the most unappreciated aspects of Reagan's intellectual evolution is the place that Chambers's memoir, *Witness*, held in Reagan's estimation."[46] Kengor recognizes that the spiritual dimension dominated Chambers's assessment and repudiation of Communism. Chambers clearly said as much in his famous introduction to the book *Letter to My Children* when he argued that "economics is not the central problem of this century. It is a relative problem which can be solved in relative ways. Faith is the central problem of this age. The Western world does not know it, but it already possesses the answer to this problem—but only provided that its faith in God and the freedom He enjoins is as great as Communism's faith in Man."[47]

Early in the Cold War, Chambers presented the proposition that the conflict between the Soviet Union and the West was fundamentally a spiritual conflict between atheistic Communism and the Judeo-Christian tradition. Chambers saw no room for accommodation between the two sides. The conflict would result in victory for one side and defeat for the other. Détente and containment were foreign concepts to Chambers; the battle was fundamentally spiritual, with evil defeating good or good defeating evil. Small wonder, then, as Kengor notes, that "throughout *Witness*, Chambers used the word evil frequently to describe Soviet Communism."[48] The evil nature of Communism and the necessity of defeating it were two core elements in *Witness* that would find a correspondence with Reagan's views toward Communism during the 1950s and beyond. Professors Paul Kengor and Ted McAllister agree that the spiritual dimension within the book particularly influenced Reagan's views toward Communism. As McAllister himself notes, "Reagan was influenced by *Witness*, especially by Chambers's description of two competing faiths, which suggested a greater cosmic and spiritual struggle behind the geopolitics."[49]

Although Reagan had largely developed his hard-line views toward Communism by the time *Witness* was published in 1952, the book still had a powerful influence on him and helped reinforce his views toward Communism. Chambers's book clearly articulated the journey of a former Communist toward a new understanding that Communism was evil and could not be tolerated; it had to be defeated. This view was shared by other conservative intellectuals as well. Perhaps the most notable was James Burnham, another former Communist and a New York University philosophy professor with degrees from Princeton and Oxford. Burnham went on to publish a variety of works during the 1950s, also calling for the defeat of Communism.

Reagan read *Witness* several years after his difficult and dangerous experience with Communists in Hollywood. Peter Schweizer notes that "Reagan had picked up the book on a recommendation from a friend, and decades later he would be able to quote passages from memory."[50] Interestingly, a number of Reagan administration speechwriters have independently and separately described Reagan's memorization of various passages from *Witness*.[51] Further, many of Reagan's presidential addresses included lines cited from *Witness*, and Reagan continued to keep copies of the book many years after its original 1952 publication. On February 21, 1984, Reagan awarded Chambers the Presidential Medal of Freedom posthumously—a fitting tribute to an intellectual who had influenced the thought of millions of Americans, including the fortieth president of the United States.

The Road to Serfdom

Credible evidence strongly suggests that Reagan read a condensed version of Friedrich A. Hayek's *The Road to Serfdom* in 1945 or 1946. One of the leading books derived from the libertarian vein of the emerging postwar conservative movement, *The Road to Serfdom* advanced political and economic arguments to assault the growing worldwide movement toward centralized planning and socialism. The book was part of the broader conservative reaction against collectivism.

William Pemberton has noted that, "after World War II, libertarian, traditional, and anti-Communist conservatives, sharing the same core beliefs, cooperated in an uneasy alliance. . . . To libertarians, the 1930s represented the rise of big government, to traditional conservatives it was the decade of nihilism and mass society, and to the anti-Communists it was, simply, the Red Decade."[52] The three conservative factions would unite in confronting a common enemy, and the libertarians would be led by the Austrian economists who would revive the arguments of nineteenth-century classical liberalism, and contribute some original arguments of their own, to resist "what seemed an inexorable movement toward collectivism."[53] Friedrich A. Hayek's book *The Road to Serfdom* would lead this libertarian charge.

Hayek (1899–1992) has been described as "perhaps the foremost philosopher of libertarianism during the twentieth century."[54] Hayek was born in Austria and was educated at the University of Vienna. He studied with Ludwig von Mises in the Austrian tradition of economics, which traced its legacy through Carl Menger to Adam Smith and the classical liberalism of the nineteenth century. Hayek was not an anarchist, nor did he argue for laissez-faire capitalism. Rather, he argued in support of limited government for the protection of political and economic freedom; nevertheless, he "sanctioned a considerable positive role for government. He allowed many welfare state provisions of social services by government, including in education, health care, unemployment and retirement insurance, and public charity, among many others."[55] However, like Nobel Prize winning economist Milton Friedman, Hayek was concerned about a government monopoly of social welfare services and advocated volunteerism and privatization to limit government's role in society. Hayek emphasized the "rule of law" throughout society rather than governmental direction, control, and "moral" compulsion.[56]

Hayek left Austria for England in 1931 and took a professorship in economics at the London School of Economics (LSE). It was at LSE that Hayek wrote *The Road to Serfdom*, which was published in 1944. Six years later, Hayek took a position at the University of Chicago with other leading intellectuals, including Milton Friedman. The University of Chicago is well known for its history of Nobel Prize winning economists, and Hayek contributed to that legacy by winning a Nobel Prize in economics in 1974. His other works included *The Constitution of Liberty* (1960); *Law, Legislation, and Liberty* (1979); and *The Fatal Conceit: The Errors of Socialism* (1988), his last major publication. Ebenstein notes that "during his later years, Hayek was an intellectual inspirer for many in the Reagan and Thatcher governments."[57]

Hayek's best-known work, however, was *The Road to Serfdom*. Hayek wrote this book while teaching at the London School of Economics and watching the gathering crisis of what would become World War II. Hayek would advance several key arguments in his book, but as Ebenstein has stated, "[Hayek] insightfully argued that not only is a socialist economy inherently unproductive, it is intrinsically despotic."[58] Hayek's book presented a compelling critique of centralized economic planning in which he persuasively argued that elites directing a national economy had "cognitive limitations" that would impair economic efficiency and impoverish the nation. Moreover, individual liberty would be threatened by centralized economic planning since "economic control is not merely control of a sector of human life which can be separated from the rest; it is the control of the means for all our ends."[59] Hayek was particularly concerned that England would move toward greater centralized economic planning following World War II, and his polemic was intended as a warning to his adopted country.

Since *The Road to Serfdom* was a provocative argument, the response was quite strong in both England and the United States, stirring up controversy and debate. Moreover, the book did not circulate exclusively among scholars. Its core ideas found their way into key journals and magazines for the reading public on both sides of the Atlantic. Although Hayek had not written the book for the general public, the public demand for the book greatly exceeded expectations, especially in the United States. Of course reviews were mixed in their assessment of Hayek's book, but many reviews recognized the landmark quality of the book. They were right—*The Road to Serfdom* has become a classic in the economic and political literature of the twentieth century.

It is established among Reagan scholars and biographers that Ronald Reagan was well acquainted with the basic arguments presented by Hayek in *The Road to Serfdom* by the time Reagan ran for the presidency. In his book *The Age of Reagan*, Steven Hayward notes that "Lee Edwards, author of an early biography of Reagan, recalls being once left alone in Reagan's study while then-Governor Reagan went to the kitchen to prepare cocktails. Edwards began browsing Reagan's bookshelves, and was astonished to find dense works of political economy by authors such as Ludwig von Mises and Friedrich Hayek heavily underlined and annotated in Reagan's handwriting."[60] Reagan himself acknowledged his intellectual debt to Hayek in a 1981 speech to the Conservative Political Action Conference, and Peggy Noonan included Hayek in her list of Reagan's intellectual heroes.[61] However, though Reagan had likely read *The Road to Serfdom* by the time he was governor of California, the question remains just how early Reagan read the book and whether the book contributed to his political development during the 1950s. This is a difficult question to answer. To my knowledge, very few of the major Reagan biographers clearly establish a linkage between Hayek's *The Road to Serfdom* and Reagan's emerging views about political economy during the late 1940s and through the 1950s. A major exception is Lee Edwards. The author of an early biography on Reagan in 1967, Edwards argues that Reagan read a condensed version of *The Road to Serfdom* in *Reader's Digest* not long after the book's publication in 1944.[62] Edwards' view is supported by George Nash's observation that shortly after *The Road to Serfdom* was published in 1944, "the *Reader's Digest* eagerly condensed the book for its readers and arranged for the Book-of-the-Month Club to distribute more than a million reprints."[63] Hayek's book appeared for the first and only time in the *Reader's Digest* April 1945 issue. Since Reagan was a diligent reader of the *Digest* at that time, he would likely have read the condensed version of *The Road to Serfdom*.

However, the key question is, what influence, if any, did Hayek's book have on Reagan's political development? To my knowledge, there is very little evidence to conclusively answer this question. We do know, however, that Reagan continued to support Democratic candidates until 1952 and the New Deal until 1955 or 1956. Reagan's reading of Hayek apparently did not have an immediate effect on his thinking but perhaps remained latent until his later experiences with General Electric. He may also have reread the work during the 1950s. In any case, Reagan's views on political economy became much more compatible with Hayek's during Reagan's employment with General Electric. We must conclude, therefore, that Hayek's *The Road to Serfdom* served to reinforce Reagan's changing views on domestic political economy during the 1950s. *The Road to Serfdom* probably had less influence on Reagan's political development during the 1950s than did Chambers's book *Witness*, but nevertheless Reagan came to many of the same conclusions that Hayek did about the deleterious effects of centralized economic planning on a nation. Three major areas of agreement between Hayek and Reagan are palpable and would become important principles articulated by Reagan for almost forty years. The common points follow:

1. Extremist ideologies, such as Communism and Fascism, are fundamentally the same. They represent the elevation of the state at the expense of individual liberty. Hayek and Reagan both used the generic term collectivism in describing extremist ideologies that expanded the state's power and threatened individual liberty. In his famous "Time for Choosing" speech, Reagan referred to the "choice" as one of "up" or "down" rather than left or right.
2. Liberty is lost not all at once but gradually. Both Hayek and Reagan believed that the gradual expansion of the state was part of a process that, if left unchecked, would result in totalitarian government.
3. There are strong moral and economic reasons for letting individuals plan their own lives rather than allowing greater state control by government elites. For both Hayek and Reagan, government elites lacked both the moral standing and sufficient knowledge to effectively plan and control the economic decisions that would otherwise be made by individuals for themselves.

What Reagan Learned from Intellectuals

Although Reagan's political development during the 1950s was derived primarily from his experiences with Communism in Hollywood and his later employment with General Electric, his exposure to a number of journals, magazines, and books helped to reinforce and solidify his view that American freedom was threatened both from abroad and from within. Many of the articles and books Reagan read were written by intellectuals, such as Whittaker Chambers and Friedrich Hayek. These two intellectuals, in particular, had an enormous impact on the nascent conservative movement of the 1950s.

Chambers and Hayek both provided intellectual credibility to the political, economic, and spiritual views increasingly becoming part of Reagan's beliefs and values through the 1950s. But beyond this, Reagan would take some assurance in knowing that, as his views hardened against Communism and he distanced himself from liberalism and the New Deal, he was not an anomaly among attentive, learning Americans. Many political transformations like Reagan's occurred during the 1950s, including many dramatic ones. After all, Whittaker Chambers and many former Communists had described their own personal journeys after more thoroughly learning about and then escaping the evils of Communism. Friedrich Hayek shared a similar story. Although Hayek's ideological journey was not as far as Chambers's, Hayek informed his readers in his preface to *The Road to Serfdom* that "I am always told by my socialist colleagues that as an economist I should occupy a much more important position in the kind of society to which I am opposed—provided, of course, that I could bring myself to accept their views. I feel equally certain that my opposition to these views is not due to their being different from those with which I have grown up, since they are the very views with which I held as a young man and which have led me to make the study of economics my profession."[64] Hayek had been a socialist in his youth, but his study and learning—especially his learning of economics under Ludwig Von Mises—led him to repudiate socialism and adhere instead to classical liberalism or libertarian beliefs.

It is unclear whether Reagan knew about Hayek's journey from socialism to classical liberalism. In any case, Reagan knew of many intellectuals, such as Chambers, Koestler, Burnham, and others, who had traveled an even longer distance than Hayek by repudiating Communism and waging a militant campaign against it. This obviously provided some degree of support and credibility to Reagan's own political development, reflected in his hard-line position against Communism by the early 1950s. In a very real sense, Reagan would be able to identify with and understand the political and economic "journeys" of various intellectuals. After all, Reagan had been and continued to be on a journey himself.

Chambers's message in *Witness* emphasized the spiritual nature of freedom and its threatened extinction by Soviet Communism. Hayek's message in *Serfdom* was a scholarly yet practical economic and political argument in support of individual freedom and against centralized economic planning. Reagan strongly agreed with and included both intellectual messages within his own unique message about freedom, which he then delivered for almost forty years to America and to the world.

Notes

1. Dinesh D'Souza, *Ronald Reagan: How an Ordinary Man Became an Extraordinary Leader* (New York: Free Press, 1997), 14.

2. Hugh Heclo, "Ronald Reagan and the American Public Philosophy," in *The Reagan Presidency: Pragmatic Conservatism and Its Legacies*, ed. W. Elliot Brownlee and Hugh Davis Graham (Lawrence: University Press of Kansas, 2003), 18.

3. Ibid.

4. Steven F. Hayward, *The Age of Reagan: The Fall of the Old Liberal Order, 1964–1980* (New York: Random House, 2001), xxii.

5. Peter J. Wallison, *Ronald Reagan: The Power of Conviction and the Success of His Presidency* (Boulder, CO: Westview Press, 2003), 34.

6. Kiron Skinner, Annelise Anderson, and Martin Anderson, eds., *Reagan, In His Own Hand* (New York: Free Press, 2001), xv.

7. Ibid., xii.

8. Kiron Skinner, Annelise Anderson, and Martin Anderson, eds., *Reagan: A Life in Letters* (New York: Free Press, 2003), xiii.

9. Kiron Skinner, Annelise Anderson, and Martin Anderson, eds., *Reagan, In His Own Hand*, xii.

10. Lou Cannon, *President Reagan: The Role of a Lifetime* (New York: Simon & Schuster, 1991), 133.

11. Kiron Skinner, Annelise Anderson, and Martin Anderson, eds., *Reagan, A Life In Letters*, x.

12. Peter J. Wallison, *Ronald Reagan: The Power of Conviction and the Success of His Presidency*, 85.

13. Lou Cannon, *President Reagan: The Role of a Lifetime*, 138.

14. Ibid., 137.

15. Ibid., 138.

16. Howard Gardner, *Leading Minds: An Anatomy of Leadership* (New York: Harper Collins, 1996), 43, emphasis in original.

17. John B. Judis, "Smarter Than You Think," *The Nation*, January 15, 1983, 57.

18. Ibid., 56.

19. See Fred Greenstein's *The Reagan Presidency: An Early Assessment* (Baltimore, MD: Johns Hopkins University Press, 1983) and James David Barber's *The Presidential Character: Predicting Performance in the White House* (Englewood Cliffs, NJ: Prentice Hall, 1985).

20. Robert Nisbet, "The Conservative Renaissance in Perspective," *The Public Interest* 81 (Fall 1985): 131, emphasis added.

21. Tevi Troy, *Intellectuals and the American Presidency* (New York: Rowman & Littlefield, 2002), 142.

22. William A. Rusher, *The Rise of the Right* (New York: William Morrow, 1984), 33.

23. George H. Nash, *The Conservative Intellectual Movement in America Since 1945* (New York: Basic Books, 1976), xiii.

24. Ibid.

25. Ibid.

26. Ibid.

27. Ibid.

28. Robert Nisbet, "The Conservative Renaissance in Perspective," *The Public Interest* 81 (Fall 1985): 132.

29. Ibid., 133.

30. Kiron Skinner, Annelise Anderson, and Martin Anderson, eds., *Reagan: A Life in Letters*, 7.

31. Ibid., 8.

32. Lou Cannon, *President Reagan: The Role of a Lifetime*, 293–94.

33. Ibid., 280.

34. Ibid.

35. See, especially, Ted V. McAllister's "Reagan and the Transformation of American Conservatism" in *The Reagan Presidency: Pragmatic Conservatism and Its Legacies*, ed. W. Elliot Brownlee and Hugh Davis Graham (Lawrence: University Press of Kansas, 2003); John B. Judis's "Smarter Than You Think," *The Nation*, January 15, 1983; and Lou Cannon's *Governor Reagan: His Rise to Power* (New York: Public Affairs, 2003), 123.

36. Kiron Skinner, Annelise Anderson, and Martin Anderson, eds., *Reagan: A Life in Letters*, 281.

37. Interview with Lee Edwards on February 10, 2004.

38. Ted V. McAllister, "Reagan and the Transformation of American Conservatism," in *The Reagan Presidency: Pragmatic Conservatism and Its Legacies*, ed. W. Elliot Brownlee and Hugh Davis Graham (Lawrence: University Press of Kansas, 2003), 51.

39. George H. Nash, *The Conservative Intellectual Movement in America Since 1945*, 148.

40. Gregory Schneider, "Right Then," *Weekly Standard*, September 23, 2002, 33.

41. Peter Schweizer, *Reagan's War*, 20.

42. Ibid., 21.

43. Ibid.

44. William A. Rusher, *The Rise of the Right*, 33.

45. George H. Nash, *The Conservative Intellectual Movement in America Since 1945*, 103.

46. Paul Kengor, *God and Ronald Reagan: A Spiritual Life* (New York: Regan Books, 2004), 76.

47. Whittaker Chambers, *Witness* (New York: Random House, 1952), 17.

48. Paul Kengor, *God and Ronald Reagan: A Spiritual Life*, 81.

49. Ted V. McAllister, "Reagan and the Transformation of American Conservatism," 51.

50. Peter Schweizer, *Reagan's War*, 32.

51. In an interview with Lee Edwards on February 10, 2004, Mr. Edwards described how Anthony Dolan, a speechwriter for Reagan, once described how Reagan recited to him lines memorized from *Witness*. Former speechwriters Peter Robinson and William Muir validate the same point.

52. William E. Pemberton, *Exit with Honor: The Life and Presidency of Ronald Reagan* (New York: M. E. Sharpe, 1997), 45–46.

53. Ibid., 46.

54. William Ebenstein and Alan Ebenstein, *Great Political Thinkers*, 6th ed. (Belmont, CA: Wadsworth, 2000), 814.

55. Ibid., 817.

56. Ibid., 818.

57. Ibid., 819.

58. Ibid., 816.

59. Ibid.

60. Steven F. Hayward, *The Age of Reagan: The Fall of the Old Liberal Order, 1964–1980*, xxii.

61. Peggy Noonan, *When Character Was King: A Story of Ronald Reagan* (New York: Viking Press, 2001), 146.

62. Interview with Lee Edwards on February 10, 2004. Edwards also thinks Barry Goldwater read *The Reader's Digest* condensed version at about the same time.

63. George H. Nash, *The Conservative Intellectual Movement in America Since 1945*, 7.

64. Friedrich A. Hayek, *The Road to Serfdom* (Chicago: University of Chicago Press, 1944), vi.

~

CHAPTER SIX

The Journey and Its Meaning

Ronald Reagan is among that handful of American politicians, and a much smaller group of presidents, who have conducted their careers primarily as a struggle about ideas. . . . One could go further and say that Reagan was probably the only twentieth century president whose political career was so thoroughly devoted to contesting for the public philosophy. To appreciate this significance, one must pay as much attention to Reagan's pre-presidential years as to his White House years.

—Hugh Heclo

Ronald Reagan's journey from Democrat to Republican is not simply an interesting biographical segment of his life. Yes, it is that, but it is much, much more. If we understand the key influences that contributed to Reagan's political development between 1945 and 1962, we also deepen and enrich our understanding of significant elements of the Reagan presidency. For, although Reagan's presidency came eighteen years after he switched from the Democratic to the Republican Party, the public philosophy he learned during his sojourn, and the priorities that philosophy advanced, remained the same throughout his political career and guided his presidency. As political scientist Hugh Heclo has recognized, Reagan was unique among presidents in being so thoroughly devoted to advancing his public philosophy from the Oval Office, which originated when he began his political sojourn from Democrat to Republican in 1945. That public philosophy was coherent and fully developed by 1960. In that year, Reagan was ready to join the Republican Party and promote the presidential candidacy of Richard Nixon. The Nixon team, however, told him that "he would be more effective if he campaigned for their man as a Democrat."[1] Reagan would change his party registration from Democrat to Republican in 1962, and in 1966, he would launch his political career by running for governor of California. He would continue to champion his public philosophy, but now he would do it as a contender for, and a successful holder of, high public office.

After his gubernatorial years, Reagan would have six years between 1974 and 1980 to further hone and refine his public philosophy. The core remained the same: America was founded on freedom, freedom was being threatened (mainly by Soviet Communism and expansion of the federal bureaucracy), and freedom required protection. During his wilderness years between 1974 and 1980, Reagan developed, without fundamentally changing, his public philosophy. He "founded a political action committee called Citizens for the Republic, wrote a syndicated newspaper column, recorded a daily radio commentary, and gave speeches for a living. . . . He read widely, looking not for a new philosophy but for ammunition for his views."[2] He continued reading *National Review* and *Human Events,* but he also read or reread the works of Hayek and Solzhenitsyn during this time frame. These activities further refined the public philosophy he had learned years earlier.

The public philosophy Reagan learned during his sojourn years of 1945 to 1962 became the "Reagan Message" in the 1980 presidential campaign. Reagan's electoral victory over Jimmy Carter brought this message to the forefront of public discourse throughout the country. This was a unique occasion. Presidential scholars have observed that most presidents do not have a well-defined and coherent public philosophy. They are generally pragmatists that hold to a number of policy positions they consider important. Reagan was different. For instance, Blessing and Skleder argue that "with the possible exceptions of Jefferson and Theodore Roosevelt, no president ever entered the White House so fully politically defined [as Reagan]."[3] Commenting along similar lines, former Reagan official Peter Wallison argues that Reagan "sought the presidency to implement a set of firmly held ideas about government's proper role that he—virtually alone among major public figures at the time he ran—believed."[4] As Reagan himself said in his second autobiography, "I'd come to Washington to put into practice ideas I'd believed in for decades."[5]

According to Heclo, "Just as Communist power represented the external threat, modern government expansion represented the internal threat to America's consecrated mission of freedom."[6] This was the heart of Reagan's public philosophy. It would become the foundation for his presidential agenda. This argument is also advanced by Andrew Busch in his book *Ronald Reagan and the Politics of Freedom*. Busch persuasively argues that the Reagan presidency was defined largely by its successful efforts to enlarge American freedom. To Busch, the Reagan foreign and domestic policy agendas were grounded in Reagan's public philosophy, and, as Busch himself has noted, "to Reagan, freedom was the most fundamental American principle, the cause that allowed individuals to make America great."[7]

A Focused Presidency and the Bully Pulpit

In his widely acclaimed book about the Reagan presidency, *Revolution*, Martin Anderson, a top economic adviser to Reagan, recalls the 1980 presidential campaign and Reagan's emphasis on the importance of priorities for winning the election and for governing afterward. According to Anderson, "Reagan was thinking out loud about President Carter's disastrous performance during the preceding four years. 'The problem with Carter,' said Reagan, 'is that he tries to do everything at once and he tries to do too much of it himself. If we win we are going to set priorities and do things one at a time.' And [according to Anderson] that is exactly what Reagan did when he was elected, and it was probably the wisest thing he did as president."[8]

As president, Reagan had two priorities derived from his public philosophy. According to Anderson, "The first was to rebuild America's military strength. The second was to rebuild America's economic strength. All other issues, important as they might be, were rigorously relegated to the sidelines."[9] Rebuilding America's military strength was an important priority for countering the Soviet threat to American freedom. Rebuilding America's economic strength would also strengthen American freedom at home, particularly by reducing the federal tax and regulatory role in domestic affairs.

Because Reagan brought a coherent public philosophy to the presidency, he was able to advance his priorities effectively through consistent and well-defined speeches to the American people and to members of his administration. Reagan proved to be one of the most successful of modern presidents in using his office as a bully pulpit from which to exercise moral leadership. He regarded the presidency as "a place to which Americans looked for hope and from which he was determined to shape the ways they thought about themselves, their society, and their government. And he loved fulfilling that purpose."[10]

Because educating the American people on both domestic and foreign policy issues was very important to Reagan, he intentionally devoted himself more than most presidents to the speechwriting process. Moreover, he consciously delegated administrative duties in order to focus his own attention on the articulation of his ideas to the American people. This was an intentional decision on Reagan's part rather than a manifestation of laziness or incompetence. Reagan did what he thought was most important for the nation at the time: He attempted to change its public philosophy. William Muir, a former speechwriter to Vice President George H. W. Bush and a professor at the University of California at Berkeley, says that "the picture of Reagan that [Garry] Wills and [Lou] Cannon (and even David Stockman) ultimately offered was of a man who cared passionately about, and worked untiringly at, making a public argument. Reagan, they agreed, sought to organize the White House so that the routines of managing the U.S. government were delegated to individuals with whom he was in tune. He sought to conserve his personal energies for making his public argument, changing people's minds, and sowing his philosophy in the hearts of the people."[11]

Reagan's Presidential Effectiveness

Books have been and will continue to be written about Ronald Reagan's presidential effectiveness. That has not been the focal point of this book. However, Reagan's journey from Democrat to Republican had enormous significance beyond the time frame of his journey, from 1945 to 1962. In fact, the journey was perhaps the greatest of all influences that defined the Reagan presidency.

Scholars, however, have had difficulty evaluating the effectiveness of the Reagan presidency. One major impediment to the current scholarship on the Reagan presidency has been the application of an anachronistic standard in evaluating his presidential effectiveness. This standard is not necessarily obsolete, but it is inapplicable in evaluating the Reagan presidency. Developed decades ago by several prominent presidential scholars, most notably by Harvard presidential scholar Richard Neustadt, this conventional model was largely derived from the successful attributes of Franklin Roosevelt's presidency and then applied to his successors in the Oval Office.

The Neustadt model of presidential effectiveness places a premium on the president's ability to gather information, assess his power stakes, learn and master policy detail, and continuously bargain with and persuade others in order to get his way. FDR's presidency helped establish the precedent for this model. However, a growing number of critics have argued, and will continue to argue, that the model does not apply in evaluating the effectiveness of the Reagan presidency. As John Sloan notes, "Obviously Reagan's success could not be attributed to Richard Neustadt's recommendation that a president should be his own political intelligence adviser, tenaciously seeking information which will give the necessary advantage in bargaining situations."[12] Other scholars have also recognized the limitations of the Neustadt model in evaluating the effectiveness of the Reagan presidency.[13] Even Neustadt himself acknowledges the special challenge the Reagan presidency presents to his model.[14] Clearly, new criteria are needed to fairly and impartially evaluate the effectiveness of the Reagan presidency. These criteria should include various measures of Reagan's successful use of the "bully pulpit" in his attempt to shape the American public philosophy according to the lessons he had learned during his journey from Democrat to Republican decades earlier.

Perhaps one important measure of Reagan's success in emphasizing the bully pulpit during his presidency was that he came to be called the "Great Communicator." And in his Farewell Address to the Nation, Reagan evaluated his own presidential effectiveness in this role when he observed with humility, "In all of that time, I won a nickname, 'The Great Communicator.' But I never thought it was my style or the words I used that made a difference. It was the content. I wasn't a great communicator, but I communicated great things, and they didn't spring full bloom from my brow, they came from the heart of a great nation—from our experience, our wisdom, and our belief in the principles that have guided us for two centuries. They called it the Reagan revolution. Well, I'll accept that, but for me it always seemed more like the great rediscovery, a rediscovery of our values and our common sense."[15] And, according to one prominent political scientist, Reagan's message about the great rediscovery of American values constituted a *story* about American identity that distinguished Reagan from most other twentieth-century presidents. Hugh Heclo has argued that "unlike most other twentieth-century American politicians, there will be a fixedness to Reagan that is somewhat immune to contemporary circumstances. This is because so much of his public presence subsisted in a story, the master narrative he had to tell about America into which all his other stories fit. The power of the story helped insulate him politically in his time and will probably do the same in the future. For it was, and will be, not simply the man but the power of the story that any critic has to overcome."[16]

Heclo has captured the core of the Reagan story to America when he states, "Looking at the elements of Reagan's story, we have found some very powerful features: the sacramental vision of a reality beyond or, perhaps better, within the obvious visible realm; innocence and its mission against evil; the struggle of a nation of individuals to escape from governmental attacks on their freedom; . . . perhaps even the consolation that while humans may fall, God will assure that His plan comes right in the end."[17]

An important measure of Reagan's presidential effectiveness will, to a significant degree, be judged by the endurance of his American story in the hearts and minds of future Americans. That Reagan's success was already evident the year he left office was proclaimed by Senator Edward Kennedy (D-MA). One of the leading opponents to Reagan's public philosophy and policy positions, Kennedy delivered a speech at Yale University in March 1989 in which he said, "Whether we agree with him or not, Ronald Reagan was an effective president. He stood for a set of ideas. . . . He meant them, and he wrote most of them not only into public law but into the national consciousness."[18]

If Kennedy is right, then Ronald Reagan was not just simply the Great Communicator but perhaps the Great Educator as well. He attempted to educate the American people about its first principles of freedom and limited government for over forty years. General Electric plants, community organizations, political rallies, domestic and foreign capitals, and a host of other forums were his classrooms. Although he mastered the techniques of public speaking, he always considered the content of his message to be most important. His message changed little after he completed his journey from Democrat to Republican, but his political career would provide a much larger audience for his message. In his Farewell Address, Reagan said, "As long as we remember our first principles and believe in ourselves, the future will always be ours. And something else we learned: Once you begin a great movement, there's no telling where it will end. We meant to change a nation, and instead, we changed a world."[19] The change Reagan spoke about came largely through his effective use of the bully pulpit. However, the Great Educator at one time had to be educated himself. For over a decade and a half after World War II, Reagan struggled to make sense of the world in a journey that took him from the Democratic to the Republican Party. That journey, culminating in a strong and compelling story about America, has become an important key to understanding the uniqueness of the Reagan presidency and its legacy to America and the world.

Notes

1. Dinesh D'Souza, *Ronald Reagan: How an Ordinary Man Became an Extraordinary Leader* (New York: Free Press, 1997), 62.

2. Ibid., 75.

3. Tim H. Blessing and Anne A. Skleder, "Top Down: A General Overview of Present Research on Ronald Reagan's Doctrinal Presidency," in *Reassessing the Reagan Presidency*, ed. Richard S. Conley (New York: University Press of America, 2003), 34n67.

4. Peter J. Wallison, *Ronald Reagan: The Power of Conviction and the Success of His Presidency* (Boulder, CO: Westview Press, 2003), 35.

5. Ronald Reagan, *An American Life* (New York: Simon & Schuster, 1990), 287.

6. Hugh Heclo, "Ronald Reagan and the American Public Philosophy," in *The Reagan Presidency: Pragmatic Conservatism and Its Legacies*, ed. W. Elliot Brownlee and Hugh Davis Graham (Lawrence: University Press of Kansas, 2003), 29.

7. Andrew E. Busch, *Ronald Reagan and the Politics of Freedom* (Lanham, MD: Rowman & Littlefield Publishers, 2001), xviii.

8. Martin Anderson, *Revolution: The Reagan Legacy* (Stanford, CA: Hoover Institution Press, 1990), 56–57.

9. Ibid., 57.

10. William Ker Muir, Jr., *The Bully Pulpit: The Presidential Leadership of Ronald Reagan* (San Francisco: ICS Press, 1992), 2.

11. William Ker Muir, Jr., *The Bully Pulpit*, 12.

12. John W. Sloan, "The Decision-Making Styles of Two Reconstructive Presidents: Franklin Roosevelt and Ronald Reagan," in *Reassessing the Reagan Presidency*, ed. Richard S. Conley, p. 126.

13. Tim Blessing and Anne Skleder reviewed a significant amount of research on the Reagan presidency and determined that "in many ways, Reagan served as a standing rebuttal to the 'standard model' of presidential performance as it had been promulgated by Neustadt and his interpreters." Tim Blessing and Anne A. Skleder, "Top Down: A General Overview of Present Research on Ronald Reagan's Doctrinal Presidency," in *Reassessing the Reagan Presidency*, ed. Richard S. Conley, 24. Peter Wallison makes the same argument throughout his book *Ronald Reagan: The Power of Conviction and the Success of His Presidency*.

14. Peter J. Wallison, *Ronald Reagan: The Power of Conviction and the Success of His Presidency*, 6.

15. Ronald Reagan, "Farewell Address to the Nation," in *Speaking My Mind* (New York: Simon & Schuster, 1989), 412.

16. Hugh Heclo, "Ronald Reagan and the American Public Philosophy," in *The Reagan Presidency: Pragmatic Conservatism and Its Legacies*, ed. W. Elliot Brownlee and Hugh Davis Graham, 36.

17. Ibid.

18. Dinesh D'Souza, *Ronald Reagan: How an Ordinary Man Became an Extraordinary Leader*, 228.

19. Ronald Reagan, "Farewell Address to the Nation," in *Speaking My Mind*, 413.

Index

Reagan, Nelle, 4, 9–12, 64, 66, 68
Reagan, Ronald W.: core beliefs, 9–11; employment with GE, 44–49; family and friends (1940s), 60–77; family and friends (1950s), 77–83; intelligence, 87–91; journey of life, 1–8; learned about Communism, 29–35; learned about encroaching federal government, 51–54; learned from family and friends, 83–84; learned from intellectuals, 103–5; presidency, 111–14; reading, 95–103
Roosevelt, Franklin D. (FDR), 4–5, 12–14, 23, 39–40, 42–43, 45, 59, 61, 67–68, 70, 72–73, 75–76, 80, 82–83, 112

Schultz, George, 89–90
Schweizer, Peter, 18–19, 24–25, 27, 31–32, 97, 99
Screen Actors Guild (SAG), 24–28, 30, 33, 41, 45, 60–61, 73–74, 76
socialist, 91, 93, 101, 104

Sorrell, Herb, 24, 28
Soviet Union, 17–18, 21–22, 42–43, 68, 98–99
speechwriting, 112
spiritual, 8, 98–99, 104
Stevenson, Adlai, 34

Thatcher, Margaret, 101
traditionalists, 93
Truman, Harry, 34, 42–43
Tullock, Gordon, 49–50
tyranny, 30, 53–54

Venona, 18

Wallace, Henry, 23, 34, 42–43
Warner Brothers, 21, 25, 42, 76
Weaver, Richard, 93–94
Willkie, Wendell, 5, 75
Wills, Garry, 14, 26, 28, 64–65, 69, 112
Winthrop, John, 4
Wyman, Jane, 13, 24, 27, 61–62

~

About the Author

Edward M. Yager is an associate professor of political science at Western Kentucky University, where he teaches courses on the American presidency, American political thought, American politics, and political theory. His publications have examined government ethics, economic development, and privatization issues. He has been invited as an Academic Visitor to the London School of Economics and Political Science, where he will research Reagan and Thatcher speeches on public management reform. He earned his Ph.D. in political science from the University of California at Santa Barbara in 1993.